THE MOUNTAIN BIKER'S GUIDE TO
SOUTHERN NEW ENGLAND

Dennis Coello's America by Mountain Bike Series

THE MOUNTAIN BIKER'S GUIDE TO SOUTHERN NEW ENGLAND

---

*Dennis Coello's America by
Mountain Bike Series*

*Massachusetts
Connecticut
Rhode Island*

Paul Angiolillo

Foreword and Introduction
by Dennis Coello, Series Editor

MENASHA
RIDGE
PRESS

Library of Congress Cataloging-in-Publication Data

Angiolillo, Paul.
   The mountain biker's guide to southern New England :
Paul Angiolillo ; foreword and introduction by Dennis Coello,
series editor. — 1st ed.
   p.   cm.
   — (Dennis Coello's America by mountain bike series)
   ISBN 1-56044-221-2
   1. All terrain cycling—New England—Guidebooks.
2. New England—Guidebooks. I. Title. II. Series:
America by mountain bike series.
GV1045.5.N36A54   1993
917.4'0443—dc20   93-32404
                                            CIP

Maps by Tim Krasnansky
Cover photo by Michael Giannaccio/New England Stock Photo

Menasha Ridge Press
3169 Cahaba Heights Road
Birmingham, Alabama 35243

Falcon Press
P. O. Box 1718
Helena, Montana 59624

   Text pages printed on recycled paper.

Table of Contents

WARNING

Outdoor recreation activities are by their very nature potentially hazardous. All participants in such activities must assume the responsibility for their own actions and safety. The information contained in this guidebook cannot replace sound judgment and good decision-making skills, which help reduce risk exposure, nor does the scope of this book allow for disclosure of all the potential hazards and risks involved in such activites.

Learn as much as possible about the outdoor recreation activities you participate in, prepare for the unexpected, and be safe and cautious. The reward will be a safer and more enjoyable experience.

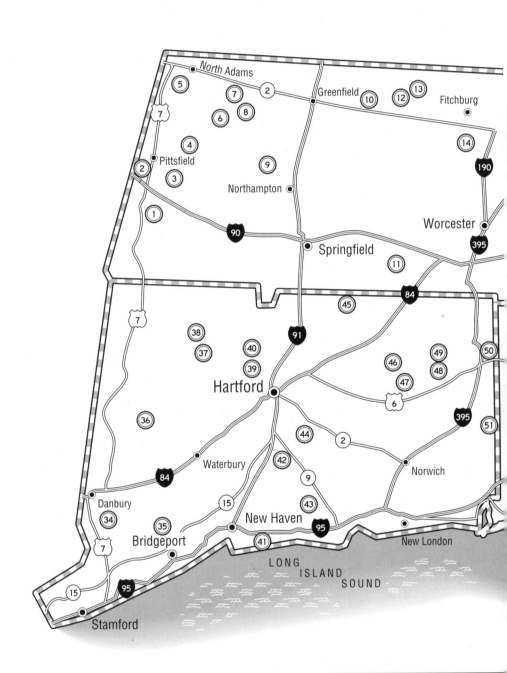

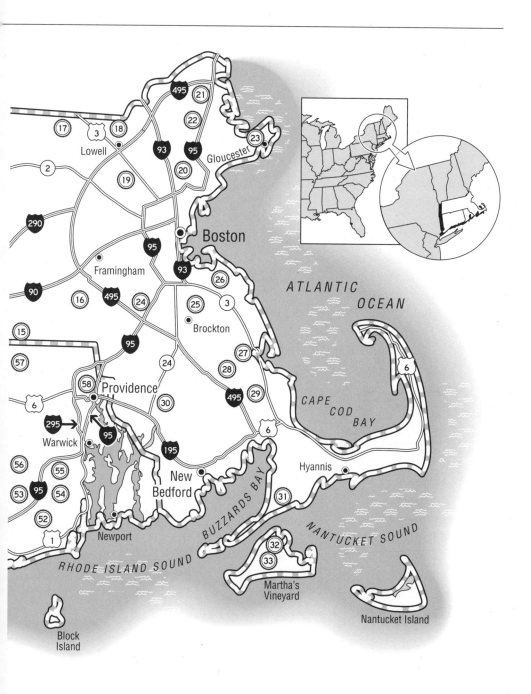

List of Maps

AMERICA BY MOUNTAIN BIKE *MAP LEGEND*

Ride trailhead

Steep grade

Primary bike trail	Direction of travel	(arrows point downhill)	Optional bike trail and trailhead	Other trail	Hiking trail

Interstate highways (with exit no.)	U.S. routes	State routes	Beartown Rd. Other paved roads	Unpaved, gravel or dirt roads (may be 4WD only)

U.S. Forest Service roads	Boston ◉ Hartford Cities	North Adams ◉ Provincetown Towns or settlements	Dam Lake	River, stream or canal

0 ½ 1
MILES

Approximate scale in miles

N

True North

MAUDSLAY ST. PK.

Parklands

State Border

- ✈ Airport
- ▼ Archeological or historical site
- ·) Archery range
- ▲ Campground (CG)
- ≡ Cattle guard
- ✝ Cemetery or gravesite
- ♠ Church
- Cliff, escarpment or outcropping
- Drinking water

- Fire tower or lookout
- Food
- Gate
- House or cabin
- Lodging
- Mountain or butte
- Mountain pass
- ⚠ Mountain summit
  3312 (elevation in feet)
- Military test site
- ✗ Mine or quarry

- Museum
- Observatory
- Park office or ranger station
- ⅂ Picnic area
- Port of Entry
- Power line or pipeline
- Horse farm or stable
- Swimming Area
- Transmission towers
- Tunnel or bridge

Foreword

Welcome to *America by Mountain Bike,* a twenty-book series designed to provide all-terrain bikers with the information necessary to find and ride the very best trails everywhere in the mainland United States. Whether you're new to the sport and don't know where to pedal, or an experienced mountain biker who wants to learn the classic trails in another region, this series is for you. Drop a few bucks for the book, spend an hour with the detailed maps and route descriptions, and you're prepared for the finest in off-road cycling.

My role as editor of this series was simple: First, find a mountain biker who knows the area and loves to ride. Second, ask that person to spend a year researching the most popular and very best rides around. And third, have that rider describe each trail in terms of difficulty, scenery, condition, elevation change, and all other categories of information which are important to trail riders. "Pretend you've just completed a ride and met up with fellow mountain bikers at the trailhead," I told each author. "Imagine their questions, be clear in your answers."

As I said, the *editorial* process—that of sending out riders and reading the submitted chapters—is a snap. But the work involved in finding, riding, and writing about each trail is enormous. In some instances our authors' tasks are made easier by the information contributed by local bike shops or cycling clubs, or even by the writers of local "where-to" guides. Credit for these contributions is provided in each chapter, and our sincere thanks goes to all who have helped.

But the overwhelming majority of trails are discovered and pedaled by our authors themselves, then compared with dozens of other routes to determine if they qualify as "classic"—that area's best in scenery and cycling fun. If you've ever had the experience of pioneering a route from outdated topographic maps, or entering a bike shop to request information from local riders who would much prefer to keep their favorite trails secret, or know how it is to double- and triple-check data to be positive your trail info is correct, then you have an idea how each of our authors has labored to bring about these books. You and I, and all the mountain bikers of America, are the richer for their efforts.

Dennis Coello
Salt Lake City

P.S. You'll get more out of this book if you take a moment to read the next few pages explaining the "Trail Description Outline." Newcomers to mountain biking might want to spend a minute, as well, with the Glossary, so that terms like *hardpack, single-track,* and *windfall* won't throw you when you come across them in the text. "Topographic Maps" will help you understand a biker's need for topos and tell you where to find them. And the section titled "Land-Use Controversy" might help us all enjoy the trails a little more. Finally, though this is a "where-to," not a "how-to" guide, those of you who have not traveled the backcountry might find "Hitting the Trail" of particular value. All the best.

Preface

by *Paul Angiolillo*

People have been cutting trails and building woods roads in Massachusetts, Connecticut, and Rhode Island for about 400 years. Native Americans were the first pathfinders, followed by European settlers in the 1600s. Later, conservationists donated large tracts of private land to create the first public parks and forests. In the 1930s, the Civilian Conservation Corps, a federal work project, built hundreds of miles of unpaved roads on public lands.

All this trailblazing activity means that nowadays you will find dozens of nearby mountain bike rides no matter where you live or visit in southern New England. There are gentle excursions on scenic roads, whoop-de-doo rides on twisting, looping trails, and everything in between. Furthermore, I can't think of another activity that covers so much ground (so to speak) at once. You can enjoy nature, get a good workout, appreciate historical regions, and have a lot of fun.

Before you head for the hills (or deep woods or countryside), here's a bit of information about local bike shops, state government agencies, mountain biking groups, and other resources in the area.

First, literally hundreds of bike shops—many of them specializing in mountain biking—are tucked away in small towns in southern New England. They're an invaluable source of information about local riding areas, group rides, trail maps, and of course repairs and supplies. I mention them under individual rides.

Throughout this book I also cite the three state agencies that manage most parks and forests in this region, and also describe them in the introduction to each state. As is happening in other regions, state parks and forests in southern New England seem perpetually threatened by budget cuts, which translates into smaller staffs to assist visitors, the closing of camping areas and swimming beaches, and fewer trail maps. (Fortunately, the trails themselves are never "closed.") Mountain bikers can help simply by using these public recreational areas, as well as supporting them with modest camping and swimming fees.

Another general observation about riding in this region is that some rides, notably in eastern Massachusetts, use compact networks of trails. These intricate "spaghetti" configurations are a lot of fun, for they offer long rides in geographically small areas, or short simple rides if you prefer. Still, negotiating these trail systems successfully can mean riding there more than once, or doing a day's exploration, or hooking up with a group ride. Remember, if all mountain bike rides were straightforward the sport wouldn't be half as much fun.

Mountain biking can be an elevating activity. Pennwood State Park, Simsbury, Connecticut.

MASSACHUSETTS

Many of the best mountain bike sites in Massachusetts can be found in state forests and parks, run by the Department of Environmental Management (DEM). There are almost 150 DEM areas, ranging from the modest, 476-acre Maudslay State Park in Newburyport, with a gentle network of well-maintained trails (Ride #21), to the 16,021-acre October Mountain State Forest in Berkshire County. The latter has miles and miles of rugged, secluded old woods roads and multi-use trails (Ride #3).

The DEM distributes free trail maps of many of its forests and parks through the Division of Forests and Parks, 100 Cambridge Street, Boston, MA 02202, (617) 727-3180; and also offers the "Massachusetts Forest and Parks" map listing all of its parks and forests, their facilities, and contact phone numbers. Another DEM map covers camping sites. For updated information on a particular DEM park or forest, you might also contact one of five regional headquarters: Southeast (508) 644-5522, Northeast (508) 887-5931, Worcester County (508) 368-0126, Connecticut River Valley (413) 545-5993, and Berkshires (413) 499-4263.

Trail Access in DEM Parks and Forests

As in other states, Massachusetts park managers are still developing policies about mountain biking. Currently, riding is allowed on all unpaved roads and double-track trails; single-track riding is permitted at the discretion of local park managers. In practice, most single-track trails are open for biking, or else restrictions apply only to certain trails designated for hiking, horseback riding, or environmental protection (like pond shorelines). If you're not sure whether to ride on a trail, ask the local rangers. They'll appreciate it.

Other Resources

To keep abreast of group rides, local races, trail clean-up parties, and other mountain bike news, there's the New England Mountain Bike Association, 69 Spring Street, Cambridge, MA 02141, (617) 497-6891. It has a phone line with riding information (PRO4MTN), and also puts out a newsletter. For a $10 membership, it's worth your support.

Some outdoor sporting goods stores are a good source of maps, including topographical ones. There's a Recreation Equipment, Inc. (REI) outlet in Reading, just off Route 128 north of Boston, (617) 944-5103. A good map and book store in Harvard Square, the Globe Corner Bookstore, specializes in topographical maps, and maps and books about New England. You'll find it at 49 Palmer Street, Cambridge, MA 02138, (617) 497-6277.

For group rides in eastern Massachusetts, check out the Friday *Boston Globe* sports section, which lists them.

The Eastern Massachusetts Bike Map, which shows several dozen mountain biking areas, is available in many bike shops and outdoor stores for $4.95, or by mail for $5.20 from Bike Maps Massachusetts, P.O. Box 1035 Porter Branch, Cambridge, MA 02140.

CONNECTICUT

This state rivals its neighbor to the north for its devotion to public trails. Connecticut is also somewhat stricter about where mountain biking is allowed, possibly because it's a smaller state and close to New York City.

Officially, mountain biking is not allowed on a 500-mile network of *blue-blazed* trails, the oldest trail system in the country, which crisscrosses both public and private land. In practice, however, local park and forest managers decide if riding is allowed on these trails, as well as other single-track trails. In some parks, some trails are clearly more suited to hiking, while in other areas trails are secluded, underused, and wide and flat.

The Department of Environmental Protection (DEP) manages all state parks and forests in Connecticut. It provides trail maps of some of its parks and forests. You may order them from: DEP, Bureau of Parks and Forests, 165 Capital Avenue, Hartford, CT 06106, (203) 566-2305. For camping information call (203) 566-2304.

For more information about trails in the Nutmeg State, there's the Connecticut Forest and Parks Association, a private organization that publishes the highly popular *Connecticut Walk Book,* now in its 17th edition. You can order this book of trails from them at 16 Meriden Road, Rockfall, CT 06481, (203) 346-2372. The cost is $17.

Local mountain bike advocates meet monthly as the Mountain Bike Committee, which is part of the Coalition of Connecticut Bicyclists. You can contact them at P.O. Box 121, Middletown, CT 06457.

RHODE ISLAND

State-maintained forests in Rhode Island are called "management areas," because they were originally created as game preserves for hunting. Today, these largely undeveloped areas are used by plenty of hikers, horseback riders, and mountain bikers, as well as hunters in the late fall and early winter. They're attractive, scenic sites for biking. For information about hunting seasons, contact the Division of Fish and Wildlife, Wakefield, RI 02879, (401) 789-3094, or (401) 277-3075.

The state has an excellent, up-to-date map of all highways and byways, including unpaved routes. For a copy, contact the Tourism Bureau at (800) 556-2484, or if calling from Rhode Island, (401) 277-2601. This bureau also mails out brochures on many recreational activities and sites, including camping, accommodations, attractions, events, boating, fishing, and maps of Newport and Block Island.

The most active local mountain biking group is the Rhode Island Fat Tire Club (245 Old Coach Road, Charlestown, RI 02877, (401) 364-0786). It sponsors group rides, including one at the favorite local riding site of Arcadia Management Area (Ride #53 in this book). Arcadia has its own information number: (401) 539-2356. After you've done an inland trail or two in the Ocean State, head a few miles east or south and enjoy the coast. You'll love the scenic and riding diversity in Rhode Island, and throughout southern New England.

Acknowledgments

Doing this book was not a solo effort. The Bicycle Exchange in Cambridge, Massachusetts, supplied me with many necessities of the trail, and the Globe Corner Bookstore in Cambridge and Boston donated maps and guidebooks.

Four people showed me multiple rides: Scott Holmes, Bill "the Old Coot" Boles, Mike Morris, and Jim Hoard. Several dozen other kind souls also made this book possible. Thanks to the following:

Bill Couch
Tom Spano
Theo Stein
Wayne Sakal
John Peipon
Steve Merlino
Jared Strand
Tom Boyden
Pete Schaefer
Monica Cazzetta
Geoff Jones
Tom Gallagher
Mike LaChance
Bob Richard
Joan Olson
Wendi Flower
Don Ploss
Bob Morse
Ruth Wheeler

Paul Rinehart
Bob Hatton
Phil Remillard
Bruce Romano
Phil Getchell
Jim Godin
Lloyd Crawford
Cliff and Ruth
Danny O'Brien
Doug Jensen
Joe Sloane
George Record
Jon Simmons
Matt Theroux
Scott Hirtle
Lester Peterson
Bill Aldrich
Michael O'Connor

Introduction

TRAIL DESCRIPTION OUTLINE

Information on each trail in this book begins with a general description that includes length, configuration, scenery, highlights, trail conditions, and difficulty. Additional description is contained in eleven individual categories. The following will help you understand all of the information provided.

Trail name: Trail names are as designated on USGS (United States Geological Survey) or Forest Service or other maps, and/or by local custom.

Length: The overall length of a trail is described in miles, unless stated otherwise.

Configuration: This is a description of the shape of each trail—whether the trail is a loop, out-and-back (that is, along the same route), figure-eight, trapezoid, isosceles triangle, or if it connects with another trail described in the book.

Difficulty: This provides at a glance a description of the degree of physical exertion required to complete the ride, and the technical skill required to pedal it. Authors were asked to keep in mind the fact that all riders are not equal, and thus to gauge the trail in terms of how the middle-of-the-road rider—someone between the newcomer and Ned Overend—could handle the route. Comments about the trail's length, condition, and elevation change will also assist you in determining the difficulty of any trail relative to your own abilities.

Condition: Trails are described in terms of being paved, unpaved, sandy, hard-packed, washboarded, two- or four-wheel-drive, single-track or double-track. All terms that might be unfamiliar to the first-time mountain biker are defined in the Glossary.

Scenery: Here you will find a general description of the natural surroundings during the seasons most riders pedal the trail, and a suggestion of what is to be found at special times (like great fall foliage or cactus in bloom).

Highlights: Towns, major water crossings, historical sites, etc., are listed.

General location: This category describes where the trail is located in reference to a nearby town or other landmark.

Elevation change: Unless stated otherwise, the figure provided is the total gain and loss of elevation along the trail. In regions where the elevation variation is not extreme, the route is described in a more general manner of flat, rolling, or as possessing short steep climbs or descents.

Season: This is the best time of year to pedal the route, taking into account trail condition (for example, when it will not be muddy), riding comfort (when the weather is too hot, cold, or wet), and local hunting seasons.

Note: Because the exact opening and closing dates of deer, elk, moose, and antelope seasons often change from year to year, it is suggested that riders check with the local Fish and Game department, or call a sporting goods store (or any place that sells hunting licenses) in a nearby town. Wear bright clothes in fall, and don't wear suede jackets while in the saddle. Hunter's-orange tape on the helmet is also a good idea.

Services: This category is of primary importance in guides for paved-road tourers, but is far less crucial to most mountain bike trail descriptions because there are usually no services whatsoever to be found. Authors have noted when water is available on desert or long mountain routes, and have listed the availability of food, lodging, campgrounds, and bike shops. If all these services are present, you will find only the words "All services available in. . . ."

Hazards: Special hazards like steep cliffs, great amounts of deadfall, or barbed-wire fences very close to the trail are noted here.

Rescue index: Determining how far one is from help on any particular trail can be difficult due to the backcountry nature of most mountain bike rides. Authors therefore state the proximity of homes or Forest Service outposts, nearby roads where one might hitch a ride, or the likelihood of other bikers being encountered on the trail. Phone numbers of local sheriff departments or hospitals have not been provided because, again, phones are almost never available. Besides, if a phone is reached the local operator will connect you with emergency services.

Land status: This category provides information regarding whether the trail crosses land operated by the Forest Service, Bureau of Land Management, a city, state, or national park, whether it crosses private land whose owner (at the time the author did the research) allowed mountain bikers right of passage, and so on.

Note: Authors have been extremely careful to offer only those routes that are open to bikers and are legal to ride. However, because land ownership changes over time, and because the land-use controversy created by mountain bikes still has not subsided totally, it is the duty of each cyclist to look for and to heed signs warning against trail use. Don't expect this book to get you off the hook when you're facing some small-town judge for pedaling past a "Biking Prohibited" sign erected the day before. Look for these signs, read them, and heed the advice. And remember there's always another trail.

Maps: The maps in this book have been produced with great care, and in conjunction with the trail-following suggestions will help you stay on course. But as every experienced mountain biker knows, things can get tricky in the backcountry. It is therefore strongly suggested that you avail yourself of the detailed information found in the 7.5 minute series USGS (United States Geological Survey) topographic maps. In some cases, authors have found that specific Forest Service or other maps may be more useful than the USGS quads, and tell how to obtain them.

Finding the trail: Detailed information on how to reach the trailhead, and where to park your car is provided here.

Sources of additional information: Here you will find the address and/or phone number of a bike shop, governmental agency, or other source from which trail information can be obtained.

Notes on the trail: This is where you are guided carefully through any portions of the trail that are particularly difficult to follow. The author also may add information about the route that does not fit easily into the other categories.

ABBREVIATIONS

The following road-designation abbreviations are used in the *America by Mountain Bike* series:

CR	County Road
FR	Farm Route
FS	Forest Service road
I-	Interstate
IR	Indian Route
US	United States highway

State highways are designated with the appropriate two-letter state abbreviation, followed by the road number. *Example:* UT 6 = Utah State Highway 6.

Postal Service two-letter state code:

AL	Alabama	KS	Kansas
AK	Alaska	KY	Kentucky
AZ	Arizona	LA	Louisiana
AR	Arkansas	ME	Maine
CA	California	MD	Maryland
CO	Colorado	MA	Massachusetts
CT	Connecticut	MI	Michigan
DE	Delaware	MN	Minnesota
DC	District of Columbia	MS	Mississippi
FL	Florida	MO	Missouri
GA	Georgia	MT	Montana
HI	Hawaii	NE	Nebraska
ID	Idaho	NV	Nevada
IL	Illinois	NH	New Hampshire
IN	Indiana	NJ	New Jersey
IA	Iowa	NM	New Mexico

NY	New York	TN	Tennessee
NC	North Carolina	TX	Texas
ND	North Dakota	UT	Utah
OH	Ohio	VT	Vermont
OK	Oklahoma	VA	Virginia
OR	Oregon	WA	Washington
PA	Pennsylvania	WV	West Virginia
RI	Rhode Island	WI	Wisconsin
SC	South Carolina	WY	Wyoming
SD	South Dakota		

TOPOGRAPHIC MAPS

The maps in this book, when used in conjunction with the route directions present in each chapter, will in most instances be sufficient to get you to the trail and keep you on it. However, these maps cannot begin to provide the detailed information found in the 7.5 minute series USGS (United States Geological Survey) topographic maps. Recognizing how indispensable these are to bikers and hikers alike, many bike shops and sporting goods stores now carry topos of the local area.

But if you're brand new to mountain biking you might be wondering, "What's a topographic map?" In short, these differ from standard "flat" maps because they indicate not only linear distance, but elevation as well. One glance at a topo will show you the difference, for "contour lines" are spread across the map like dozens of intricate spider webs. Each contour line represents a particular elevation, and each topo has written at its base a particular "contour interval" designation. Yes, it sounds confusing if you're new to the lingo, but it truly is a simple and wonderfully helpful system. Keep reading.

Let's assume that the 7.5 minute series topo before us says "Contour Interval 40 feet," and that the short trail we'll be pedaling is two inches in length on the map, and crosses five contour lines between its beginning and end. What do we know? Well, because the linear scale of this series is two thousand feet to the inch (roughly 2¾ inches representing a mile), we know our trail is approximately four-fifths of a mile long (2″ × 2000′). But we also know we'll be climbing or descending two hundred vertical feet (5 contour lines × 40 feet each) over that distance. And the elevation designations written on occasional contour lines will tell us if we're heading up or down.

The authors of this series warn their readers of upcoming terrain, but only a detailed topo gives you the information that enables you to pinpoint your position exactly on a map, steer you toward optional trails and roads nearby, plus let you know at a glance if you'll be pedaling hard to take them. It's a lot of information for a very low cost. In fact, the only drawback with topos is their size—

several feet square. I've tried rolling them into tubes, folding them carefully, even cutting them into blocks and photocopying the pieces. Any of these systems is a pain, but no matter how you pack the maps you'll be happy they're along. And you'll be even happier if you pack a compass as well.

Major universities and some public libraries also carry topos; you might try photocopying the ones you need to avoid the cost of buying them. But if you want your own and can't find them locally, write to:

USGS Map Sales
Box 25286
Denver, CO 80225

Ask for an index while you're at it, plus a price list and a copy of the booklet *Topographic Maps*. In minutes you'll be reading them like a pro.

A second excellent series of maps available to mountain bikers is that put out by the United States Forest Service. If your trail runs through an area designated as a national forest, look in the phone book (white pages) under the United States Government listings, find the Department of Agriculture heading, and then run your finger through that section until you find the Forest Service. Give them a call and they'll provide the address of the regional Forest Service office, from which you can obtain the appropriate map.

LAND-USE CONTROVERSY

A few years ago I wrote a long piece on this issue for *Sierra Magazine* and called literally dozens of government land managers, game wardens, mountain bikers, and local officials, to get a feeling for how ATBs were being welcomed on the trails. All that I've seen personally since, and heard from my authors, indicates there hasn't been much change. Which means we're still considered the new kid on the block, that we have less right to the trails than horses and hikers, and that we're excluded from many areas including:

a) wilderness areas
b) national parks (except on roads, and those paths specifically marked "bike path")
c) national monuments (except on roads open to the public)
d) most state parks and monuments (except on roads, and those paths specifically marked "bike path")
e) an increasing number of urban and county parks, especially in California (except on roads, and those areas specifically marked "bike path")

Frankly, I have little difficulty with these exclusions and would, in fact, restrict our presence from some trails I've ridden (one time) due to the environmental damage and chance of blind-siding the many walkers and hikers I met up with along the way. But these are my personal views. They should not be interpreted as those of the authors and are mentioned here only as a way to introduce the land-use problem and the varying positions on it, which even mountain bikers hold.

You can do your part in keeping us from being excluded from even more trails by riding responsibly. Many local and national off-road bicycle organizations have been formed with exactly this in mind, and one of the largest—NORBA, the National Off-Road Bicycle Association—offers the following code of behavior for mountain bikers:

1. I will yield the right-of-way to other non-motorized recreationists. I realize that people judge all cyclists by my actions.
2. I will slow down and use caution when approaching or overtaking another cyclist and will make my presence known well in advance.
3. I will maintain control of my speed at all times and will approach turns in anticipation of someone around the bend.
4. I will stay on designated trails to avoid trampling native vegetation and minimize potential erosion to trails by not using muddy trails or short-cutting switchbacks.
5. I will not disturb wildlife or livestock.
6. I will not litter. I will pack out what I pack in, and pack out more than my share whenever possible.
7. I will respect public and private property, including trail use signs, no trespassing signs, and I will leave gates as I have found them.
8. I will always be self-sufficient and my destination and travel speed will be determined by my ability, my equipment, the terrain, the present and potential weather conditions.
9. I will not travel solo when bikepacking in remote areas. I will leave word of my destination and when I plan to return.
10. I will observe the practice of minimum impact bicycling by "taking only pictures and memories and leaving only waffle prints."
11. I will always wear a helmet whenever I ride.

Now, I have a problem with some of these—number nine, for instance. The most enjoyable mountain biking I've ever done has been solo. And as for leaving word of destination and time of return, I've enjoyed living in such a way as to say, "I'm off to pedal Colorado. See you in the fall." Of course it's senseless to take needless risks, and I plan a ride and pack my gear with this in mind. But for me number nine smacks too much of the "never-out-of-touch" mentality. And getting away from civilization, deep into the wilds, is, for many people, what mountain biking's all about.

All in all, however, theirs is a good list, and surely we mountain bikers would be liked more, and excluded less, if we followed the suggestions. But let me offer a "code of ethics" I much prefer, one given to cyclists by Utah's Wasatch-Cache National Forest office.

Study a Forest Map Before You Ride
Currently, bicycles are permitted on roads and developed trails within the Wasatch-Cache National Forest except in designated Wilderness. If your route crosses private land, it is your responsibility to obtain right of way permission from the landowner.

Keep Groups Small
Riding in large groups degrades the outdoor experience for others, can disturb wildlife, and usually leads to greater resource damage.

Avoid Riding on Wet Trails
Bicycle tires leave ruts in wet trails. These ruts concentrate runoff and accelerate erosion. Postponing a ride when the trails are wet will preserve the trails for future use.

Stay on Roads and Trails
Riding cross-country destroys vegetation and damages the soil.

Always Yield to Others
Trails are shared by hikers, horses, and bicycles. Move off the trail to allow horses to pass and stop to allow hikers adequate room to share the trail. Simply yelling "Bicycle!" is not acceptable.

Control Your Speed
Excessive speed endangers yourself and other forest users.

Avoid Wheel Lock-up and Spin-out
Steep terrain is especially vulnerable to trail wear. Locking brakes on steep descents or when stopping needlessly damages trails. If a slope is steep enough to require locking wheels and skidding, dismount and walk your bicycle. Likewise, if an ascent is so steep your rear wheel slips and spins, dismount and walk your bicycle.

Protect Waterbars and Switchbacks
Waterbars, the rock and log drains built to direct water off trails, protect trails from erosion. When you encounter a waterbar, ride directly over the top or dismount and walk your bicycle. Riding around the ends of waterbars destroys them and speeds erosion. Skidding around switchback corners shortens trail life. Slow down for switchback corners and keep your wheels rolling.

If You Abuse It, You Lose It
Mountain bikes are relative newcomers to the forest and must prove themselves responsible trail users. By following the guidelines above, and by participating in trail maintenance service projects, bicyclists can help avoid closures which would prevent them from using trails.

I've never seen a better trail-etiquette list for mountain bikers. So have fun. Be careful. And don't screw up things for the next rider.

HITTING THE TRAIL

Once again, because this is a "where-to," not a "how-to" guide, the following will be brief. If you're a veteran trail rider these suggestions might serve to remind you of something you've forgotten to pack. If you're a newcomer, they might convince you to think twice before hitting the backcountry unprepared.

Water: I've heard the questions dozens of times. "How much is enough? One bottle? Two? Three?! But think of all that extra weight!" Well, one simple physiological fact should convince you to err on the side of excess when it comes to determining how much water to pack: a human working hard in ninety-degree temperature needs approximately ten quarts of fluid every day. Ten quarts. That's two and a half gallons—*twelve* large water bottles, or *sixteen* small ones. And with water weighing in at approximately eight pounds per gallon, a one-day supply comes to a whopping twenty pounds.

In other words, pack along two or three bottles even for short rides. And make sure you can purify the water found along the trail on longer routes. When writing of those routes where this could be of critical importance, each author has provided information on where water can be found near the trail—if it can be found at all. But drink it untreated and you run the risk of disease. [See *Giardia* in the Glossary.]

One sure way to kill both the bacteria and viruses in water is to boil it for ten minutes, plus one minute more for each one thousand feet of elevation above sea level. Right. That's just how you want to spend your time on a bike ride. Besides, who wants to carry a stove, or denude the countryside stoking bonfires to boil water?

Luckily, there is a better way. Many riders pack along the effective, inexpensive, and only slightly distasteful tetraglycine hydroperiodide tablets (sold under the names of Potable Aqua, Globaline, Coughlan's, and others). Some invest in portable, lightweight purifiers that filter out the crud. Yes, purifying water with tablets or filters is a bother. But catch a case of Giardia sometime and you'll understand why it's worth the trouble.

Tools: Ever since my first cross-country tour in 1965 I've been kidded about the number of tools I pack on the trail. And so I will exit entirely from this discussion by providing a list compiled by two mechanic (and mountain biker) friends of mine. After all, since they make their livings fixing bikes, and get their kicks by riding them, who could be a better source?

The following is suggested as an absolute minimum:

tire levers
spare tube and patch kit
air pump
allen wrenches (3, 4, 5, and 6 mm)
six-inch crescent (adjustable-end) wrench
small flat-blad screwdriver
chain rivet tool
spoke wrench

But their personal tool pouches carried on the trail also contain:

channel locks (small)
air gauge
tire valve cap (the metal kind, with a valve-stem remover)
baling wire (ten or so inches, for temporary repairs)
duct tape (small roll for temporary repairs or tire boot)
boot material (small piece of old tire or a large tube patch)
spare chain link
rear derailleur pulley
spare nuts and bolts
paper towel and tube of waterless hand cleaner

First-aid kit: My personal kit contains the following, sealed inside double zip-lock bags:

sunscreen
aspirin
butterfly-closure bandages
band-aids
gauze compress pads (a half-dozen 4″ × 4″)
gauze (1 roll)
ace bandages or Spenco joint wraps
Benadryl (an antihistamine to guard against possible allergic reactions)
water purification tablets
moleskin/Spenco "Second Skin"
hydrogen peroxide/iodine/Mercurochrome (some kind of antiseptic)
snakebite kit

Final considerations: The authors of this series have done a good job in suggesting that specific items be packed for certain trails—like raingear in particular seasons, a hat and gloves for mountain passes, or shades for desert jaunts. Heed their warnings, and think ahead. Good luck.

Dennis Coello
Salt Lake City

MASSACHUSETTS

Western Massachusetts

RIDE 1 · BEARTOWN STATE FOREST

This moderately challenging eight-mile loop ride explores several secluded trails in this 11,000-acre forest in the heart of scenic Berkshire County. The ride is actually made up of three interconnecting shorter loops. First, you will climb for a mile or so on a rugged double-track trail, with some mud in flatter areas and loose rock and eroded areas on steeper stretches. As you climb watch how the woodscape changes from the darker, thicker, moister habitat of hardwood and softwood trees, to a sunny highland environment of smaller trees, bushes, and ferns. Then it's cruising time along single-track trails for several miles, before descending on dirt roads. Halfway along the ride, you will reach a secluded pond and the stone walls and chimney of an old house. In winter, snowmobilers and cross-country skiers use some of these trails.

To the south in the forest there's a 35-acre swimming pond with a hiking trail around it. The Appalachian Trail (known familiarly as the "AT") also runs through the forest—but it's off-limits for bicycling. During the summer, this part of Massachusetts (called "the Berkshires") attracts tourists to its peaceful landscape and many cultural attractions, including the Tanglewood Music Festival and Jacob's Pillow Dance Theater.

General location: The forest is located between the towns of South Lenox and Monterey, 4 miles south of Exit 2 on Interstate 90 (the Massachusetts Turnpike).
Elevation change: The ride climbs steadily and not too steeply for the first mile, then flattens and descends for a few miles, climbs again, and then descends for 2.5 miles. Total elevation gain is 400'.
Season: Any time between summer and late fall is good for riding here. These trails are rideable in the winter, too, if there has been little snowfall or if snowmobilers have packed them down. Expect plenty of mud in the spring.
Services: All services are available in Stockbridge and Lee (to the north), and Great Barrington (to the west). There is camping in the park (12 campsites, $8 per night, no showers).
Hazards: At the beginning of the ride the trail is somewhat eroded and can be wet. Also, watch out for occasional motorized off-road vehicles and light traffic on the steep paved descent on Beartown Road.
Rescue index: At the most you will be about 3 miles from help on secluded trails.
Land status: State forest trails and town roads.

RIDE 1 *BEARTOWN STATE FOREST*

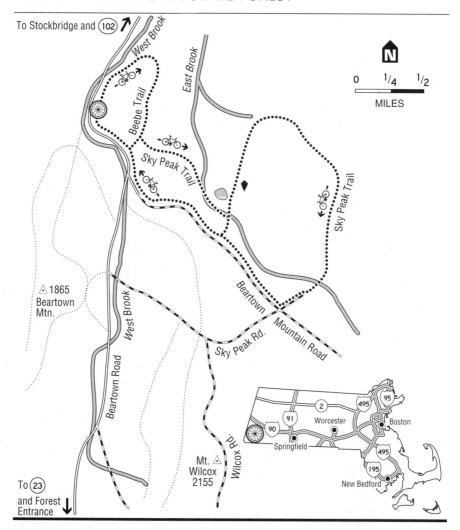

Maps: Maps may be available at the forest headquarters, or contact the Department of Environmental Management (see below).

Finding the trail: Take Exit 2 off the Massachusetts Turnpike (I-90), and head west on MA 102 toward Stockbridge. After 3 miles, follow brown signs to the left for the forest. After about 1.5 miles, you pass a large brown forest sign on the right. Soon after the sign, just before a small bridge, park at turnoffs on the right or left.

A rugged double-track trail. Beartown State Forest, Monterey, Massachusetts.

Sources of additional information:

Beartown State Forest
Blue Hill Road
Monterey, MA 01245
(413) 528-0904

Department of Environmental Management
Division of Forests and Parks
100 Cambridge Street
Boston, MA 02202
(617) 727-3180

Notes on the trail: Pick up the Beebe Trail on the eastern side of paved Beartown Road. This is the wettest and most eroded part of the ride. Climb steadily, veering to the right and following the yellow snowmobile signs. At the top of a climb, look for a single-track trail to the left. There may be a sign on a tree on the left, "Sky Peak Trail." (To do a short loop, continue straight to reach unpaved Beartown Mountain Road.) After another mile or so, you will cross a small creek and soon afterward reach a dirt road at a secluded pond. Turn left, passing the pond, and look for the stone walls and chimney of a former house on the right. (Again, you can turn right on the dirt road and reach Beartown Mountain Road.)

Just after passing the stone house, turn left to pick up the Sky Peak Trail again. (Despite its name, the Sky Peak Trail is a wooded ride.) A recent logging operation has cut a "road" straight ahead—be sure to turn left just after the pond to pick up the trail. After following the trail for several miles, curving to the right, you will come out on a wide dirt road (from another logging operation). Ride down this road to unpaved Beartown Mountain Road. (For a longer ride, continue across Beartown Mountain Road onto Sky Peak Road and then hook up with other unpaved roads and trails that eventually loop down to paved Beartown Road.) Turn right on Beartown Mountain Road and descend to paved Beartown Road. Turn right and descend to the trailhead.

RIDE 2   *JOHN DRUMMOND KENNEDY PARK*

This moderate six-mile loop ride runs through a compact, scenic, and accessible park. Just a few hundred feet from US 20 in Lenox, this quiet wooded area is full of large maple, birch, and black walnut trees, scenic areas, and the remnants of an old road and stone walls that led to the Aspinwall Hotel, a private resort that once stood near here.

As the official map of this popular area indicates, there are at least eight "points of interest" in the park, including a scenic overlook with a picnic area, a pond with benches, a large balancing rock, and a spring. The park is also a bird-watching site, and at a scenic overlook you can observe several mountain ranges, including one in New York.

The ten miles or so of trails in the park are blazed according to technical difficulty (for cross-country skiing). You can climb gently on wide double-track trails or challenge yourself on tight, steep single-track. The Main Trail is a wide, hard-packed woods road. At the other extreme, a rugged, grassy trail over a buried fiber-optic cable line crosses the park.

Lenox, in the heart of the Berkshires, is a popular vacation spot. In summer it comes alive with the Tanglewood Music Festival, the summer home of the Boston Symphony Orchestra; a world-famous dance performance shed, Jacob's Pillow Dance Theater; summer-stock theater; and film programs.

General location: The park is in Lenox on US 20.
Elevation change: The terrain is rolling, with regular short climbs and descents.
Season: Summer through late fall is the best time for riding here; avoid wet spring trails and cross-country ski tracks.
Services: All services are available in Lenox and along US 20 and US 7. There is a campground at nearby October Mountain State Forest ($12 per night, with

RIDE 2 *JOHN DRUMMOND KENNEDY PARK*

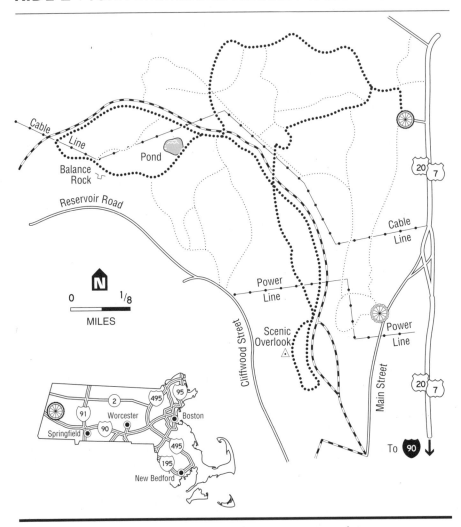

showers). To reach the campground, turn right in the center of Lee and follow the brown signs for the forest. The Arcadian Shop, a sports and bike shop in Lenox, (413) 637-3010, sponsors group rides.

Hazards: None, except for minor obstructions on the narrower trails. Also, expect to meet other park users, especially on weekends.

Rescue index: At the most you will be about a half mile from a traveled road.

Land status: Town park trails. Local mountain bikers help to maintain the trails.

Descending on a single-track trail. John Drummond Kennedy Park, Lenox, Massachusetts.

Maps: A map is available from the town of Lenox. You can pick it up at the trailhead or at the Arcadian Shop, a bike and sports store at the trailhead.

Finding the trail: Take Exit 2 off Interstate 90 (the Massachusetts Turnpike), onto US 20 West toward Lee and Lenox. Just after the road again becomes two lanes (it divides into four lanes for a short distance in Lenox), you will pass a shopping center on the left. Park there. The park is just behind the shopping center.

Sources of additional information:

Arcadian Shop
US 20
Lenox, MA 01240
(413) 637-3010

Notes on the trail: Begin in the shopping center parking lot on US 20. A double-track trail heads through a field behind the parking lot. At a four-way intersection just inside the woods there's a large trail map on a board. For a more challenging ride, follow a perimeter loop counterclockwise around the park. (At the northwest border of the park do not ride toward signs for the Audubon Sanctuary.) Most trails are marked according to their levels of difficulty.

RIDE 3   *OCTOBER MOUNTAIN STATE FOREST*

This moderate 11-mile loop ride explores just a section of this largest state forest in Massachusetts (16,021 acres), using rugged jeep roads, smoother two-wheel-drive dirt roads, and a single-track trail. This is grand and varied scenery, from sunlit highland woods with giant pine trees sweeping the sky, to trail-hugging blackberry and red raspberry bushes that produce their sweet natural snack in late August and early September. You also pass by two large lakes and a scenic overlook, and cross a dam (rebuilt in 1992).

For an easier ride, you can climb and descend on the dirt roads that intersect in the forest. For more challenging riding, there's a network of single-track trails on the western side of the forest. The official trail map labels these trails as "shared use," which means that horses and motorized off-road vehicles also use them. Local mountain bikers ride on these trails, but some of them are quite eroded and can be hard to follow.

October Mountain State Forest lies in the heart of Berkshire County, a popular vacation area in New England. Local towns such as Lenox and Becket boast many summer attractions, including the Tanglewood Music Festival (the summer residence of the Boston Symphony Orchestra), Jacob's Pillow (a world-class dance performance shed), live theater, and film programs.

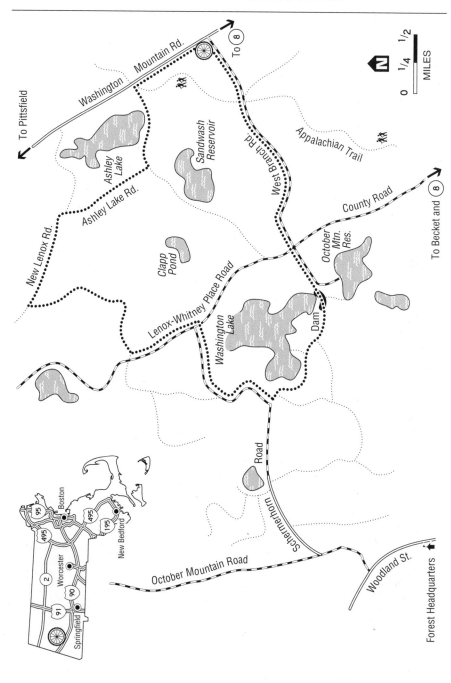

General location: This large forest is located in the towns of Lenox, Washington, and Becket, 5 miles north of Interstate 90 (the Massachusetts Turnpike) and 6 miles south of Pittsfield.

Elevation change: The ride rolls gently up and down between about 1,700' and 1,900'.

Season: Summer through late fall is the best time for riding here. There's colorful foliage in September and October.

Services: All services are available in Pittsfield, Lenox, and along US 20 and US 7. There's a campground in the forest (50 sites, $12 per night, with showers). To reach it, turn right in the center of Lee and follow the brown signs. Plaine's Bike Shop is on West Housatonic Street in Pittsfield, (413) 499-0294. The Arcadian Shop, a bike and sports store, is on US 20 in Lenox, (413) 637-3010. Weekly group rides congregate at the Arcadian Shop.

Hazards: Watch for an occasional motorized vehicle on the two-wheel-drive roads.

Rescue index: At the most you will be about 2.5 miles from help on secluded roads and trails.

Land status: State forest roads and trails.

Maps: Contact the Department of Environmental Management (DEM) for a free trail map (see below). The DEM provides maps for many state forests and parks in Massachusetts.

Finding the trail: You can reach the trailhead from either Pittsfield (to the north) or Becket (to the south). From the common in the center of Pittsfield (a lively hub city in western Massachusetts), turn east onto East Street, pass a large school, and fork right onto Elm Street. Blend left into Williams Street, and at Burgner Farm (a large farm stand with fresh foods, baked goods, and refreshments), fork right onto Washington Mountain Road. After 5 miles, turn right onto unpaved West Branch Road and park at a wide turnoff on the right (this is public land). From the south, take Exit 2 on the Massachusetts Turnpike (I-90), onto US 20 East toward Becket, and onto Washington Mountain Road heading north. You can also begin riding farther inside the forest from the junction of West Branch and County Roads. This junction can be reached from the south on County Road.

Sources of additional information:

October Mountain State Forest
Woodland Road
Lee, MA 01238
(413) 243-1778

Department of Environmental Management
Division of Forests and Parks
100 Cambridge Street

A secluded woods road. October Mountain State Forest, Washington, Massachusetts.

Boston, MA 02202
(617) 727-3180

Arcadian Shop
US 20
Lenox, MA 01240
(413) 637-3010

Notes on the trail: Ride up four-wheel-drive West Branch Road until you reach an intersection with a huge clearing on the other side of it. (Helicopters sometimes land in this clearing.) This junction is called Four Corners. (You can also begin riding here, by driving north on County Road from MA 8 in Becket.) Continue through the intersection, veering to the right on the road, and you will reach a lake and a giant dam. Take a trail across the dam and pick up a double-track trail into the woods. The dam was rebuilt in 1992. Washington Mountain Lake was drained to do it; it will take 3 years for the lake to refill completely.

Follow this rocky trail in the woods, veering to the right, and you will come out on a dirt road, Schermerhorn Road. To take a side trip, turn left and reach a trail on the right heading toward Schermerhorn Gorge, a scenic landmark. Otherwise, turn right, climb past a scenic view on the left at the height-of-land, and reach a T junction with a four-wheel-drive dirt road, Lenox-Whitney Place Road. (For an easier, shorter ride, turn right and return to Four Corners.)

Turn left onto Lenox-Whitney Place Road and, after less than a mile, turn right onto a narrower dirt road. Follow this eroded old road until it ends at the dirt New Lenox Road. Turn right, and after a mile fork right onto the abandoned Ashley Lake Road. After about another mile, turn left onto another jeep road, passing the attractive Ashley Lake on the left. You will come out on paved Washington Mountain Road, where the Appalachian Trail crosses it. (The "AT" is off-limits to cycling.) Turn right and ride back to West Branch Road.

RIDE 4 *WAHCONAH FALLS*

This easy-to-moderate five-mile loop ride circumvents a state park and then cruises through scenic countryside, mainly on two-wheel-drive dirt roads, with a mile or two on more rugged paths. After passing through a woodscape of old trees and young wildflowers, you will arrive in open countryside, with a handsome horse farm and wild raspberry bushes along the road. You'll get some exercise, though, for at the beginning and end of the ride there are climbs. At the trailhead a short, narrow trail winds down to a 40-foot falls, which spills into a swimming hole.

Nearby Pittsfield is a lively hub in western Massachusetts, with many cultural offerings. Just west of Pittsfield, on the New York state border, the huge Pittsfield State Forest (10,000 acres) has scenic overlooks and many rugged trails.

General location: This area is located just off MA 9/MA 8A, between Dalton and Windsor, about 6 miles east of Pittsfield.
Elevation change: The ride begins with a short, somewhat steep climb. Then it descends and rolls up and down before climbing back to the falls.
Season: Any time between spring and fall is good for riding here. Expect muddy terrain in early spring.
Services: All services are available along MA 9 and in Dalton.

RIDE 4 *WAHCONAH FALLS*

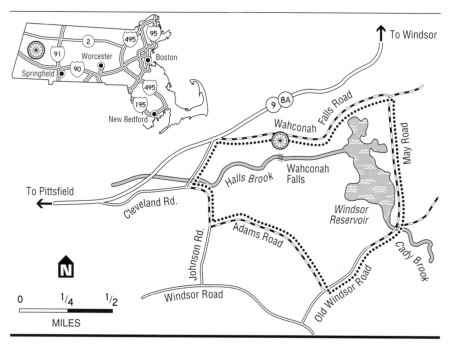

Hazards: None, except for occasional rugged sections on the four-wheel-drive roads.

Rescue index: At most you will be about a half mile from help.

Land status: Town roads and state park roads.

Maps: A detailed state or local road map will show these roads.

Finding the trail: On MA 9/MA 8A, between Dalton and Windsor, watch for brown signs for Wahconah Falls State Park. From the east, turn left onto North Street about 3.5 miles west of the junction of MA 9 and MA 8A. Then fork right onto Wahconah Falls Road and you will reach a parking lot on the right at the falls. If the lot is gated, park next to it along the road. Lock your vehicle.

Sources of additional information:

Wahconah Falls State Park
Dalton, MA 01201
(413) 442-8992

Notes on the trail: This clockwise ride is easy to follow: Turn right at all major intersections. Climb up the road through the park (passing a couple of beckoning side roads). Cross a stream and turn right at the next junction. The road will end at a "Closed" sign, but it's open to mountain bikes. Continue straight on a double-track trail and you will come out on a two-wheel-drive road near a home. Veer right, cross a bridge, veer right again, and reach a paved road.

Turn right on the paved road and, after less than a half mile, turn right again onto the narrower, unpaved Adams Road. This road becomes a jeep trail, crosses a power line (which appears to be rideable to the left), and reaches a two-wheel-drive road. Continue veering to the right and you will come out at a paved road across from a horse farm. Turn right and reach MA 9. Turn right, ride on the highway's wide shoulder for a hundred feet or so, and turn right again onto North Street. Then fork right onto Wahconah Falls Road and climb to the parking area.

RIDE 5   *MOUNT GREYLOCK STATE RESERVATION*

This challenging eight-mile loop ride runs through deep woods on abandoned old roads that have become rugged trails. The ride has some stretches of extended, technical climbing on loose rock (mainly on Cheshire Harbor Trail) and descending on severely eroded terrain (Old Adams Road and Red Gate Road). Deep in the woods, you will also ride on a single-track trail past a dramatic tree-lined gorge. A separate out-and-back ride in this 12,000-acre reservation takes a scenic two-wheel-drive dirt road to a sweeping overlook of a wilderness area.

This oldest state forest in Massachusetts surrounds the state's highest peak, 3,491-foot Mount Greylock, which today is topped with a 92-foot-high tower and summit lodge. The lodge has overnight accommodations and sponsors many events in the summer, including lectures, guided tours, and cultural events. The Appalachian Trail also runs through the reservation (although it's off-limits for biking).

Mount Greylock was one of the first state lands in Massachusetts to set aside certain trails (in 1991) for mountain biking. This ride uses three of them. The other two mountain bike trails are extremely technical. In particular, the steep Stony Ledge Trail (off Sperry Road) is a former downhill ski trail. It is treacherously "greasy" when wet. For less strenuous activities in the area, you can visit Williams College and the Clark Art Institute in Williamstown.

General location: The reservation is located in the northwest corner of Massachusetts, just south of North Adams, Williamstown, and MA 2.
Elevation change: There is a lot of climbing and descending on this ride. You'll begin at 2,350', descend to 2,000', climb again to 2,350', descend to 1,600', climb to 2,300', descend to 2,100', and climb finally to 2,400'—for a total elevation gain of 2,600'.
Season: The best riding seasons are summer and fall. There's a lot of mud in the spring.

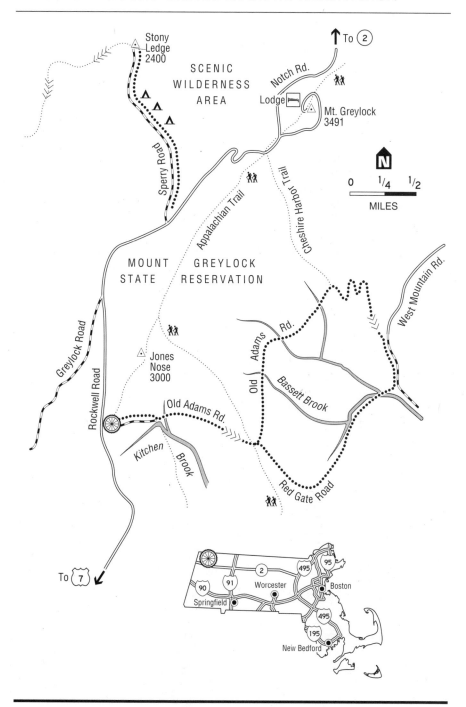

Stony Ledge 2400

SCENIC WILDERNESS AREA

To 2

Notch Rd.

Lodge

Mt. Greylock 3491

Sperry Road

Appalachian Trail

Cheshire Harbor Trail

N

0   1/4   1/2

MILES

MOUNT GREYLOCK
STATE RESERVATION

West Mountain Rd.

Greylock Road

Rockwell Road

Jones Nose 3000

Old Adams Rd.

Old Adams Rd.

Bassett Brook

Kitchen Brook

Red Gate Road

To 7

495   95
2
495
91   Worcester   Boston
90
Springfield
495
195
New Bedford

Services: All services are available in Lanesboro, North Adams, and Williamstown, including two mountain bike shops in Williamstown: The Mountain Goat on Water Street, (413) 458-8445, and The Spoke on Main Street, (413) 458-3456. There's also camping in the reservation and a good local food store at the intersection of MA 7 and MA 43.

Hazards: Watch out for severely eroded downhill stretches at the beginning of this ride and on Red Gate Road. Also, be careful on wet, rocky sections, which can be slippery.

Rescue index: At the most you will be about 3 miles from help on secluded old roads and trails.

Land status: Abandoned roads in a state forest.

Maps: Trail maps are stocked at the reservation, or contact the Department of Environmental Management (see below).

Finding the trail: You can reach the trailhead (called Jones Nose after a nearby landmark) from either MA 2 or US 7. The easiest route is from US 7 (Main Street) in Lanesboro. Follow the signs for Rockwell Road into the reservation. Fork left at the Visitor Center and continue for 3.5 miles on paved Rockwell Road, turning right into a large unpaved parking area (where a hiking trail goes to Jones Nose). You can also turn off MA 2 in North Adams, onto Notch Road, and climb on pavement for several miles over the top of Mount Greylock. Coming down the other side on Rockwell Road, turn left into the Jones Nose parking area.

Sources of additional information:

Mount Greylock State Reservation
Lanesboro, MA 01237
(413) 499-4263

The Mountain Goat
130 Water Street
Williamstown, MA 01267
(413) 458-8445
This shop has a lot of information about mountain biking in northwestern Massachusetts and across the border in New York. Several group rides begin at the shop each week.

The Spoke
618 Main Street
Williamstown, MA 01267
(413) 458-3456

Department of Environmental Management
Division of Forests and Parks
100 Cambridge Street

Panoramic view of a wilderness area. Mount Greylock State Reservation, Adams, Massachusetts.

Boston, MA 02202
(617) 727-3180

Notes on the trail: Head downhill from the parking area on Old Adams Road, which becomes heavily eroded with steep gullies. After about a half mile, just before crossing a small brook and while still going downhill, turn left at a four-way intersection and go uphill. *Note:* This is a tricky turn because you make it while still going downhill on eroded terrain. If you cross the stream you will continue on a flat single-track trail, ending up on a paved road in the neighboring town of Cheshire.

After this first turn, climb steadily and gently for almost a mile. When the trail levels off, fork sharply right onto Red Gate Road. (You can also continue on Old Adams Road for an easier, scenic out-and-back ride.) Red Gate Road climbs, veers to the left, descends, parallels and then crosses a brook, begins to climb again, and comes out at a wider trail. Turn left on this trail and climb. The trail will become wider (from a recent logging operation), will veer to the right, and then will arrive at a clearing and a two-wheel-drive road called West Mountain Road.

Take an immediate left fork into a large clearing, where there should be a sign on a tree: "Cheshire Harbor Trail." (This clearing can be another trailhead.) Climb steadily, around several switchbacks, and after about 1 mile fork left onto Old Adams Road. After 3 miles, you will pass Red Gate Road again (now on the left). Veer to the right, descend, and reenter the four-way intersection. Fork right onto the more eroded trail, and climb back to the parking area.

And for an out-and-back ride to a spectacular view: Climb Rockwell Road (northward) from the Jones Nose parking area for 1.8 miles, until you reach a scenic overlook and several directional signs at a fork. Turn left onto unpaved Sperry Road (toward the campsites). Pass the ranger station on the left (you might stop and tell a ranger that you're riding to Stony Ledge). You can also park in a public parking lot along Sperry Road. Then ride up the road for about a mile, reaching a dead end at Stony Ledge, a dramatic overlook that reveals the silent beauty of a wilderness area in this vast forest.

RIDE 6 *WINDSOR STATE FOREST*

Beginning at a swimming beach on a crystal-clear river, this ten-mile loop ride winds underneath a cathedral-like canopy of trees, passes a scenic falls, rolls through open countryside, passes an abandoned farm and a nineteenth-century cemetery . . . and that's only the first half of the ride. Less than a mile after leaving the trailhead, you pass Windsor Jambs, a series of scenic falls tumbling over water-smoothed bedrock in a shady gorge. Halfway into the ride, on Upper Road, look for wild red raspberry bushes that ripen in July and vistas through the treeline.

The terrain alternates between six miles of narrow, scenic two-wheel-drive dirt roads and four miles of rugged four-wheel-drive jeep trails. At the end of the ride, there's an optional half mile on a single-track trail. You can also swim, picnic, and camp in the forest. There is no charge to park and use the trails and roads, but swimming costs $5—and on a summer day it's well worth it.

General location: The park is in Windsor, off MA 9, about 15 miles northeast of Pittsfield.
Elevation change: You will begin riding at 1,350', will reach 1,850' after about 7 miles, and then descend back to 1,350'.
Season: Any time between spring and fall is good for riding here.
Services: There is water at the forest headquarters. All other services are available along MA 9 West.
Hazards: Be prepared for sudden changes in riding conditions from two-wheel-drive to four-wheel-drive terrain.
Rescue index: At the most you will be about 2 miles from help.
Land status: State forest roads and trails and town roads.

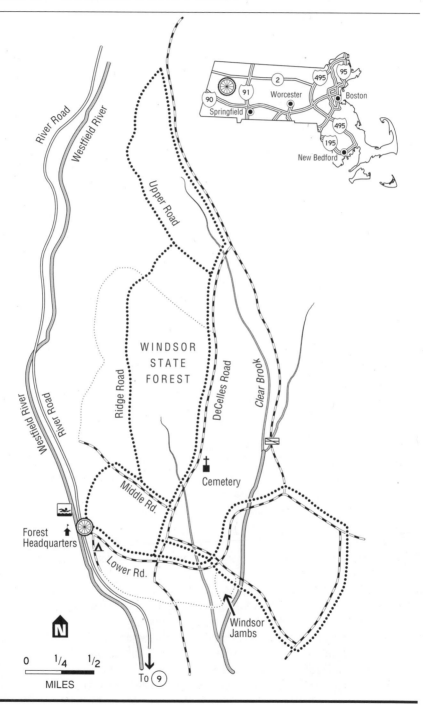

River Road

Westfield River

Upper Road

2

495

95

91

Worcester

Boston

90

Springfield

495

195

New Bedford

WINDSOR
STATE
FOREST

Ridge Road

DeCelles Road

Clear Brook

Westfield River

River Road

† Cemetery

Middle Rd.

Forest
Headquarters

Lower Rd.

Windsor
Jambs

N

0   1/4   1/2

MILES

To (9)

Maps: Maps may be available at the trailhead, or contact the state forest or the Department of Environmental Management (see below).

Finding the trail: On MA 9, about 6 miles east of Windsor, watch for brown signs for the forest. If you are heading east, turn left at a road marked "West Cummington and Windsor Jambs." After 3 miles on this paved road you will pass campsites and reach a parking lot at the forest headquarters.

Sources of additional information:

Windsor State Forest
River Road
Windsor, MA 01270
(413) 684-0948

Department of Environmental Management
Division of Forests and Parks
100 Cambridge Street
Boston, MA 02202
(617) 727-3180

Notes on the trail: This ride explores most of the trails in this forest by connecting 5 smaller loops. You can do some of the loops as shorter rides. Head across the wide stream away from the parking area, and begin climbing on gravelly Lower Road. After less than a half mile, you will cross an intersection. This is where the ride will come out (on the left). Continue straight and you'll soon reach another intersection. Turn right and you will pass Windsor Jambs on the right, a scenic falls. The road leaves the state forest, becoming a more rugged trail and going steadily downhill. It comes out on a two-wheel-drive dirt road. Turn left, veer left again, and you will reach a three-way intersection with a sign indicating a left turn toward the state forest.

Turn left (the road on the right is a dead end), and you will reenter the intersection that you passed on the way to Windsor Jambs. For a shorter ride, continue straight to return to the trailhead. Otherwise, turn right at the intersection, climb on a four-wheel-drive road, and you will reach a T junction with an abandoned farm and campsite on the other side. Turn right and pass an old cemetery on the right.

Continue climbing and watch for scenic views between trees on the right. Then, while descending, watch for a left turn onto a rugged jeep trail (Upper Road). Turn left on it and climb gently for almost a mile. You will come out on a two-wheel-drive dirt road. Turn right on it, fork right after less than a mile, and then fork right again. You're back on the road that passes the cemetery (called both Decelles Road and Windago Road).

Turn onto Upper Road again (this time it comes up on the right), and now take the first sharp left turn onto a grassy road (Ridge Road). You will reach a T junction with Middle Road at a field.

Now you can turn left, reach Decelles Road again, turn right, reach Lower

Road, and turn right toward the trailhead. Or, to take a short, challenging single-track trail, turn right onto Middle Road and watch for a trail on the left that is marked with blue blazes. This overgrown single-track trail comes out behind the camping area near the trailhead.

RIDE 7   *SAVOY MOUNTAIN STATE FOREST*

This challenging 18-mile loop ride provides more than a taste of mountain biking in western Massachusetts—it's an entire four-course meal. You will sample a mile of cross-country ski trails through a forest of red spruce, red and sugar maple, balsam, beech, and birch trees; a mile on an ungroomed single-track snowmobile trail; four miles on rugged woods roads, with a hemlock-lined side trail to a scenic falls; and nine miles on two-wheel-drive dirt roads.

From these roads run a side trail to a secluded pond, another to a balanced boulder, a steep paved road to a fire tower, rural homes, farms, a pre–Civil War cemetery, and a river gorge. About three miles of the ride also use scenic paved roads. The middle third of the loop (Tannery Road to Adams Road) can be done as a more moderate ride, with some trail-riding thrown in if you want.

The state forest offers swimming, picnicking, hiking, guided hikes, fishing, and 45 campsites (open from mid-May to mid-October). Also, several nearby state forests have trails. For cultural and intellectual stimulation, there's nearby Williamstown, home of Williams College and the Clark Art Institute, known for its collections of French Impressionist and American paintings.

General location: This ride is just southeast of North Adams, off MA 2 and MA 9.

Elevation change: You begin at 1,500', climb to 1,900', descend to 1,560', climb again to 2,220', descend to 1,000', and climb back to 1,500'—for a total elevation gain of 3,120'.

Season: Any time between late spring and late fall is good for riding here.

Services: Savoy Mountain State Forest (and several nearby state forests) have camping, restrooms, and water. There is lodging at Stump Sprouts, a guest lodge that caters to mountain bikers (see below). All other services are available in North Adams and Charlemont.

Hazards: On the wooded trails watch for fallen twigs and branches, which can snag your derailleur. On the dirt roads, watch out for the occasional motorized vehicle.

Rescue index: At the most you will be about 2 miles from help.

Land status: State forest roads and trails, public roads, and private trails with access allowed.

Maps: Stump Sprouts, a cross-country skiing and mountain biking guest lodge

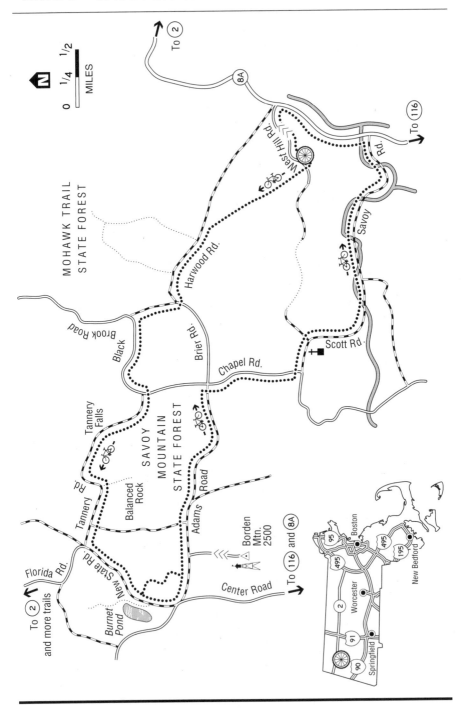

near the trailhead, offers maps. A state forest trail map is available at forest headquarters (off MA 2 to the north) or from the Department of Environmental Management (see below).

Finding the trail: From MA 2, take MA 8A south from Charlemont for 6 miles and turn right onto the steep, paved West Hill Road. After 1 mile, you will pass the Stump Sprouts guest lodge, and then a parking lot on the left. The trailhead is a grassy double-track trail just up the road from the parking lot on the right.

Sources of additional information:

Savoy Mountain State Forest
Central Shaft Road
Florida, MA 01247
(413) 663-8469

Stump Sprouts (Lloyd and Suzanne Crawford, proprietors)
West Hill Road
West Hawley, MA 01339
(413) 339-4265

Department of Environmental Management
Division of Forests and Parks
100 Cambridge Street
Boston, MA 02202
(617) 727-3180

Notes on the trail: This ride connects several loops, which can be pedaled independently. (There are also trailheads inside the state forest, along two-wheel-drive dirt roads.) To begin this ride, follow signs on a cross-country ski trail (Easy Slider Trail) uphill for about 1 mile, until you reach a three-way fork in a clearing. Turn right onto Nick's Notion Trail, then fork left, and you will reach a T junction with a narrow dirt road (the junction is named Far Corner and the road is Harwood Road).

Turn left onto the road, and after a long downhill, just as Harwood Road becomes paved, turn right onto a dirt road. (To do a shorter loop, go straight on Harwood Road and pick up the last section of this ride.) After about a half mile, you will reach an asphalt road at an open field. Turn left on the pavement, and after about a mile, just after a large field, fork right onto the narrow, unpaved Tannery Road. (Again, you can go straight to join the last section of this ride.)

You will now enter Savoy Mountain State Forest and pass a sign for Tannery Falls on the right. It's a short hike to visit the falls. After about another mile, when the road turns right uphill, you can take another side trip—a three-quarter-mile trail to Balanced Rock. (To reach it, turn left onto a double-track trail, cross a brook, and fork left.) After about another mile, you will reach the hard-packed New State Road. Turn left on it, or right for a longer ride through the state forest. After less than a mile, you will pass a brown gate on the right at

Natural arch on a cross-country ski trail. West Hawley, Massachusetts.

a double-track trail heading downhill. This short side trail reaches scenic Burnet Pond and then heads northward.

Now you can take either an overgrown snowmobile trail or continue on the two-wheel-drive road. To do some challenging single-track riding, turn left just opposite the trail heading toward Burnet Pond. After a mile on this winding, overgrown trail, you will come out on Adams Road. Otherwise, continue on New State Road until you reach a T junction, turn left, and almost immediately fork left onto unpaved Adams Road.

Then you will pass a gated, paved road on the right that climbs steeply to a fire tower on Borden Mountain. It's a tough climb. Just before this road, there's a scenic view across a field on the left. (Look for ripe raspberries in mid-July.) Then continue downhill on Adams Road, reach a four-way intersection, and turn right onto paved Chapel Road.

At the next intersection, after slightly more than a mile, turn left onto gravelly Barnard Road, pass an old cemetery on the right, veer right, and you're on Scott Road. Veer left, following the stream downhill, and you will reach paved MA 8A. (Watch out for children playing, and possibly a dog.) Turn left and ride for about 1 mile, turn left onto West Hill Road, and climb home steeply to the trailhead.

RIDE 8 *HAWLEY*

This moderate ride through both woods and open countryside combines an 8.5-mile loop and a 4-mile loop. Using two-wheel-drive and four-wheel-drive roads, the longer loop explores a forest full of pine, birch, maple, hemlock, ash, and oak trees, as well as stone walls, a wetland, a field or two, and a nineteenth-century cemetery. Finally, after three miles you will reach the village of Hawley, where you can ride past a defunct 30-foot-high brick-making kiln—and even enter it.

Then you will leave Kenneth Dubuque Memorial State Forest (commonly known as the "Hawley" state forest), pass a local swimming pond, and roll along a secluded four-wheel-drive road past a historical house (1789) and an abandoned farm site with an old apple orchard, blueberry bushes, lilies, and a good view of a nearby mountain. At the trailhead, there's a short single-track trail to the site of an old mill built over a river. It was once the site of a large tannery that kept many local citizens gainfully employed.

General location: The ride is located just south of West Hawley and MA 2, on MA 8A. Most of the ride lies in the Kenneth Dubuque Memorial State Forest.
Elevation change: At the beginning of the ride, you will climb steadily from 1,500' to 1,800'. Then it's all downhill and rolling over flat terrain.
Season: Any time between spring and fall is good for riding here.
Services: All services are available in Dalton (to the southwest), and North Adams (to the northwest).
Hazards: None, except for minor obstructions. Also, watch out for occasional vehicles on the two-wheel-drive and paved roads.
Rescue index: At most you will be about 2 miles from help on woods roads.
Land status: Old town roads and public trails, most of them in a state forest.
Maps: USGS, 7.5 minute series, Plainfield, MA.

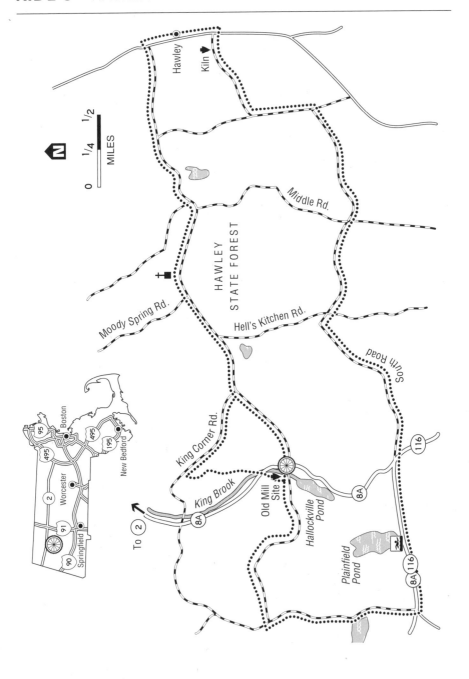

Finding the trail: On MA 8A, 1 mile north of its junction with MA 116, you pass a large brown gate at a pond on the west side of the road. If the gate is closed, park along the road near the gate, but do not block it.

Sources of additional information:

Department of Environmental Management
Connecticut River Valley Regional Headquarters
(413) 545-5993

Stump Sprouts (Lloyd and Suzanne Crawford, proprietors)
West Hill Road
West Hawley, MA 01339
(413) 339-4265

Notes on the trail: The turns and junctions on this 12.5-mile ride are distinct, but there are quite a few of them. Here's a turn-by-turn description. You can begin either on a woods road or a more challenging single-track trail past a historical mill site. To take the road, head north on MA 8A from the trailhead for a few hundred yards and turn right on a woods road. To begin the ride on the single-track trail, across a dirt road next to the pond, take a single-track trail marked, "Mill Site Trail." This is a hiking trail that requires that you carry your bike across a few stretches. You will see the old mill in the river (on the right). Keep veering right and you will reach MA 8A. Just across the highway, an overgrown opening with several wide birch log steps across it heads into the woods, at a sign reading, "Hawley Path Trail." Take this trail and almost immediately turn left in the woods, paralleling the highway.

After 1 mile on this lightly maintained trail, you will come out at a T junction on a narrow dirt road. Turn right uphill and you'll soon reach another T junction with a wider dirt road. (This is the road you can take directly from the trailhead.)

Turn left on this unpaved road, reach a pond on the right, and then fork left. (You can turn right onto another woods road, Hell's Kitchen Road, to do a shorter loop.) Next, you pass Moody Spring Road on the left, which heads north toward a spring. Then you pass a field and shelter recessed on the right and a well-maintained old cemetery.

At the next junction, turn left, and then almost immediately right at a fork and cross a small brook. (Again, you can turn right at the first junction to do a shorter loop.) After climbing some more and passing another crossroad, you go through a brown gate, leaving the state forest. Upon reaching pavement, turn right and ride through the village of Hawley. You will pass a fire station on the right, and, immediately after it, turn right into a parking area and onto a dirt road heading back into the forest.

After a short distance, you can fork right into a clearing to visit an abandoned kiln. Then continue in the other direction (west), descending on a steep hill. You will reach a T junction with a stone wall. Turn left on a more rugged road, and then right at the next junction, onto South Road. This becomes a two-wheel-drive road and comes out on MA 116. Turn right and reach the intersection of MA 116 and MA 8A.

If you want to take an additional 4-mile loop, go straight on MA 116 North/ MA 8A South. (Otherwise, turn right onto MA 8A North and ride for 1 mile back to the trailhead.) After a half mile on MA 116 North, you will pass a public beach on Plainfield Pond on the right. After another half mile, turn right onto a hard-packed dirt road heading uphill. You will pass another pond on the left, Crooked Pond, and a few homes, including a house built in 1789. After a couple of miles, you will arrive in a clearing with an abandoned orchard and a view of Borden Mountain ahead. Once past the clearing veer right, staying on the main road, and you will reach the trailhead on MA 8A.

RIDE 9   *D.A.R. STATE FOREST*

This moderately challenging five-mile ride loops through a beautiful 1,500-acre forest that's packed with scenic areas, including dramatic woodscapes and two handsome lakes. It also offers between ten and fifteen miles of trails and dirt roads. The ride uses mainly single-track trails that are rugged and steep in places, with rocks, roots, and logs to weave around or hop over. Less experienced riders can walk through the more difficult sections, or stay on the woods roads (in the eastern part of the forest).

The scenic highlight is a panoramic view of the foothills of the Berkshire Mountains from a fire tower, which you will reach by either a dirt road or a trail. Along the ride you will also pass tall evergreen and deciduous trees, mid-level mountain laurel bushes (which flower in June and July), blueberry bushes (ripening in late summer), and low-lying ferns and witch hazel. This state-managed forest (D.A.R. stands for Daughters of the American Revolution) is also a popular swimming spot, and has 50 campsites ($12 per night) with hot showers. There's also a nearby scenic area on the Westfield River on MA 9, three and a half miles west of its junction with MA 112.

General location: Goshen, off MA 112, 15 miles northwest of Northampton.
Elevation change: The ride begins by descending for 250', climbs steadily for 300', and then descends 50' to the parking area.
Season: Late spring through late fall is the best time for riding here. Expect some wetness in spring.
Services: Water, restrooms, and camping are available in the forest. All other services are in Goshen and Northhampton.
Hazards: Several trail sections are steep and obstructed so know your riding abilities. You might also lower your saddle before descending on some of the

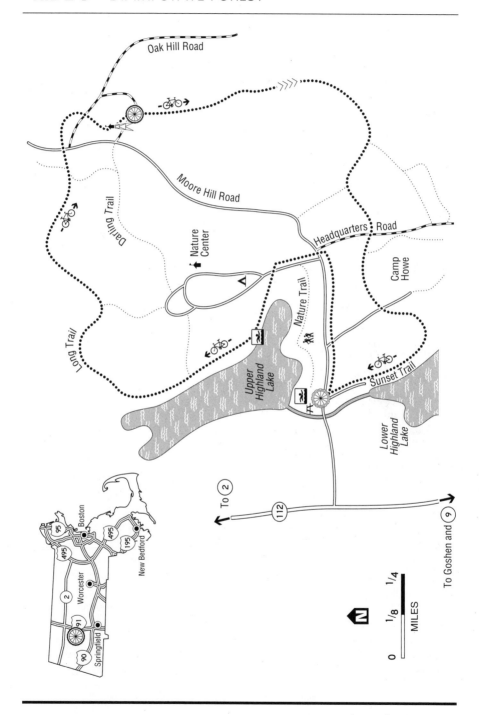

Oak Hill Road

Moore Hill Road

Headquarters Road

Darling Trail

Long Trail

Nature Center

Camp Howe

Nature Trail

Upper Highland Lake

Lower Highland Lake

Sunset Trail

Boston

New Bedford

Worcester

Springfield

To 2

To Goshen and 9

112

N

0   1/8   1/4

MILES

steeper hills. These trails are used by horseback riders and hikers, so be considerate if you encounter other users.

Rescue index: At the most you will be about 1 mile from help.

Land status: State forest trails and roads.

Maps: USGS, 7.5 minute series, Goshen, MA.

Finding the trail: On MA 112, just north of Goshen, look for brown signs for the state forest, which is on your right if coming from the south. There is a $5 fee to park and swim at the beach. If you don't plan to swim, tell the attendant that you are only using the trails. After passing the swimming beach, climb onto the paved Moore Hill Road through the forest for about a mile. At the height-of-land, turn right onto a dirt road. This is the road to the fire tower. After three-tenths of a mile, you will reach a grassy opening on the right with a sign, "Park here."

Sources of additional information:

D.A.R. State Forest
East Street
Williamsburg, MA 01096
(413) 268-7098

Department of Environmental Management
Division of Forests and Parks
100 Cambridge Street
Boston, MA 02202
(617) 727-3180

Notes on the trail: Across from and just above the parking area, pick up a single-track trail into the woods (heading south). Follow the red diamond arrows on the trees. Sometimes you must look for pieces of a marker nailed to a tree rather than an entire arrow if the marker has been broken. After the trail descends steeply, it reaches a flat area and veers to the right. Soon you will reach an intersection in the woods with arrows on four trees. Turn left, following the smaller red arrows. You will reach a dirt woods road, Headquarters Road. (For a shorter loop, you can turn right and return to Moore Hill Road.)

Then turn right on the road and almost immediately pick up the trail on the other side, now marked with a blue maple leaf. After about a half mile, you will cross a paved road leading into Camp Howe. (There is a row of water spigots at a large basin just inside the camp.) Pick up the trail on the other side of the road and you will soon reach Lower Highland Lake.

Veer right along the lake and you will come out at a paved boat launching site. Turn right on the pavement (watching out for walkers and other park users). Ride along this paved road for about a half mile, and turn left on pavement at signs for campsites and a boat ramp. Ride a short distance past the boat launching area on the left, and then fork left at a sign for the trail.

A fern-swept trail. D.A.R. State Forest, Goshen, Massachusetts.

Follow the blue trail markers across a dirt road and along the lake (Upper Highland Lake). You will pass a sign: "Long Trail to firetower, 2.3 miles." This is the trail you want. At the northern end of the lake, it veers into the woods, following blue markers (or the remains of them). After about 2 miles, fork to the left, following more signs for the fire tower. Soon you will come out at paved Moore Hill Road. You can take the trail just across the road, or the dirt road to the right of it, to reach the fire tower. Use a dirt access road heading south from the tower to return to the parking area.

Central Massachusetts

RIDE 10 *ERVING STATE FOREST*

This challenging 14-mile loop ride weaves through light woods for several miles on rugged single-track trails and steep dirt roads. Then it leaves the state forest, picking up a narrow four-wheel-drive road, a two-wheel-drive road, an overgrown single-track trail, and a short stretch on a paved road back into the forest. One can also create shorter rides out of this one. The area is full of other riding possibilities too, including more trails and old roads in four nearby state forests located in Warwick, Northfield, Erving, and Wendell.

This ride begins on an overgrown double-track trail, with bushes brushing up against you. As you descend, the habitat changes into a mature forest of full-grown trees and low-lying ferns, and then comes out at a field (full of brilliantly colored wildflowers in summer). You reenter the woods and climb to the height-of-land (look for blueberry bushes there). And that's only the first half of the ride. Laurel Lake at the trailhead has swimming at a sandy beach ($2 for biking or walking in and swimming), with a bathhouse and a concession stand.

General location: The forest is in Erving, just off MA 2, about 10 miles east of Greenfield and Interstate 91.

Elevation change: Our route includes plenty of climbing and descending. You begin at 800', climb to 1,050', descend steadily to 600', climb again to 1,100', descend to 700', climb to 900', descend to 700', and climb to 800', for a total elevation gain of 2,100'.

Season: Late spring through late fall is the best time for riding here; autumn brings bright foliage.

Services: Water and restrooms are available at Laurel Lake near the trailhead. The forest also has many campsites ($8 per night). All other services are along MA 2 and in Greenfield to the east.

Hazards: Watch out for loose terrain on some of the steeper woods roads and some hidden obstructions on the grassy, overgrown trails.

Rescue index: At most you will be about 2 miles from help.

Land status: State forest roads and trails.

Maps: Trail maps are available at the main parking lot at Laurel Lake, or contact forest headquarters (see below). (The state forest map does not show all of the trails on this ride.) Also, Erving Variety Store on MA 2 just outside the forest may carry topographical maps.

Finding the trail: Turn north off MA 2 in Erving at brown signs for the state forest. Fork right on Swamp Road, and then Laurel Lake Road, and you will

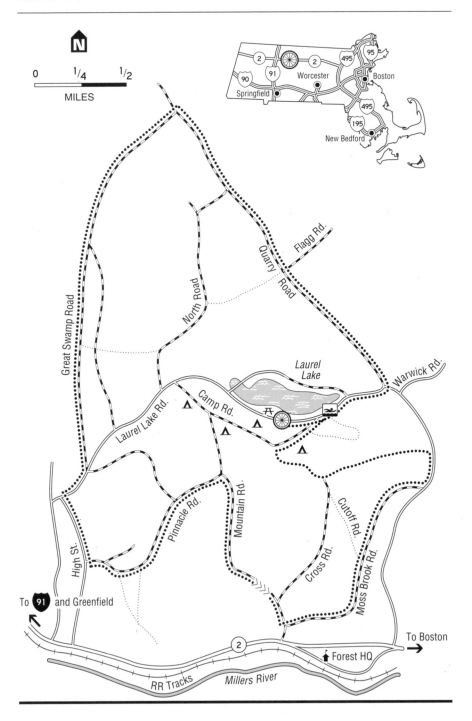

A quiet road through sunlit woods. Erving, Massachusetts.

pass Laurel Lake at 2.4 miles. There are several parking areas along the lake at picnic sites—before you reach the parking lot at the beach, which costs $5.

Sources of additional information:

Erving State Forest
Route 2
Orange, MA 01364
(508) 544-3939

Department of Environmental Management
Division of Forests and Parks
100 Cambridge Street
Boston, MA 02202
(617) 727-3180

Notes on the trail: This ride weaves in and out of the forest, using a number of secluded trails as well as dirt and paved roads. A detailed map of the area in and around the forest will be helpful.

Just before you enter the main parking lot at Laurel Lake, take a sharp right turn up steep Camp Road. After climbing for just two-tenths of a mile, you will reach the gated, overgrown Cut Off Road on the left, which heads uphill and south into the woods. Take this overgrown road, forking left at the first junction. (For a short loop, you can fork right.) Continue downhill and fork right at the next junction, onto a single-track trail. You will come out on a paved rural road near another forest parking area.

Turn right on the paved road and after less than a half mile, just before crossing a large bridge, fork right onto the gated Moss Brook Road, a grassy road heading uphill. Then veer right onto a wider, sandy road. Ride past a sand pit, veer right on the road, and you will enter a forest equipment "graveyard." Turn sharply up a steep dirt road on the right, Mountain Road.

When you begin going downhill, turn left onto Pinnacle Road, another dirt woods road. Descend for a little more than a mile, and turn right at a three-way intersection, coming out on paved High Street. Turn right onto High Street, reach a T junction with Laurel Lake Road, turn right again and, just before crossing a small bridge, fork left onto Great Swamp Road.

Follow this flat, narrow road for 2.5 miles, until it comes out on two-wheel-drive Quarry Road. After just over a mile on Quarry Road, you will pass a large brown gate at an open field on the left. You can take the trail behind the gate for an optional loop, or continue on Quarry Road.

To take the optional loop, turn left into the field and follow a grassy road past a logging clearing on the right. You'll soon reach a fork. Turn right and ride for less than a mile, coming out on dirt Flagg Road. Turn right and ride for a little more than a mile, rejoining Quarry Road. Turn left (south) on Quarry Road and descend steadily; you will soon reach an intersection with paved Laurel Lake Road. You will see a sign on it for the state forest. Turn right and climb steeply on pavement to the east side of Laurel Lake, forking left around the lake to return to the trailhead.

RIDE 11 *BRIMFIELD STATE FOREST*

This moderate 6.5-mile loop ride explores a half-dozen secluded woods roads in this sunny forest. About half of these roads are wide, flat, and hard-packed, while the other half are steeper double-track trails, with some loose rocks and protruding roots. (It's possible to do an easier loop using only the flatter, smoother roads.) Maples, ashes, and oaks share space here with stands of tall pines, and at the junction of two roads lies a large pond with an old campsite on it.

RIDE 11 *BRIMFIELD STATE FOREST*

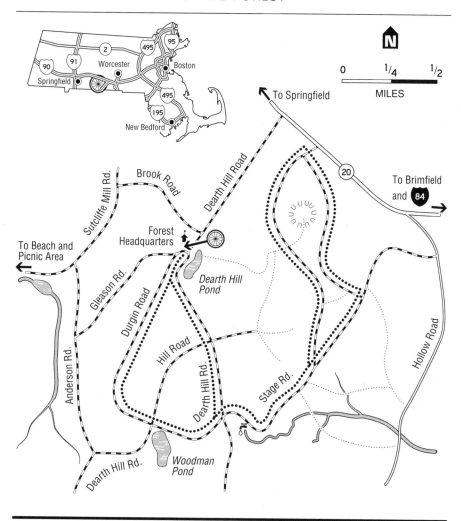

The forest also has a large picnic and swimming area, Dean Pond, on Sutcliffe Mill Road, farther along MA 20. (Although the official trail map shows no trails linking this loop to the pond, several trailheads head westward toward Sutcliffe Mill Road.) There's also an ice cream stand at a scenic dairy farm farther along MA 20 (follow the signs). Finally, this area is ten miles west of one of the most famous reconstructed Colonial-era villages in New England, Sturbridge Village, which has special public events, especially in the fall.

General location: The forest is in Brimfield, between the cities of Worcester and Springfield, and 60 miles west of Boston.

Elevation change: Although this ride is relatively flat, 2 or 3 short climbs on loose terrain will challenge you.

Season: This is a 4-season ride, if there isn't much snow. The roads are well-drained, which makes them not too muddy in the spring.

Services: All services are available along MA 20.

Hazards: Watch out for downhill stretches of loose rock and occasional minor obstructions like logs, roots, and rocks.

Rescue index: You will be about 1 mile from help on dirt roads.

Land status: Town and state forest roads.

Maps: Maps may be available at the headquarters building at the trailhead, or contact the Department of Environmental Management (see below).

Finding the trail: From Interstate 84, just a half mile south of Interstate 90 (the Massachusetts Turnpike), take Exit 8 onto MA 20 West. A couple of miles west of Brimfield, and a half mile after MA 20 becomes four-lane, turn left onto Dearth Hill Road. (If you reach a sign for the state forest, you just passed this access road.) After a half mile or so, just before a pond on the left, turn left into an unpaved parking area. The trailhead is across the road, opposite the forest headquarters.

Sources of additional information:

Department of Environmental Management
Division of Forests and Parks
100 Cambridge Street
Boston, MA 02202
(617) 727-3180

Notes on the trail: From the parking area, ride up Dearth Hill Road for a short distance and turn right into the headquarters parking area. Give a friendly wave to any rangers, and then head left (south) between two buildings, climbing on an eroded old road, Durgin Road. After 1 mile, you will reach a four-way inter-section with Hill Road. Head straight across it and past Woodman Pond on the right. (You can take a side trail around the pond, which becomes overgrown after about a half mile.)

You will intersect another dirt road, and make a dogleg turn to the left and right across it, onto Stage Road. When you reach a small fork in the trail, stay to the right. (The steep road on the left is where this ride comes out.) At the next junction, after about a half mile, turn left onto another woods road, and almost immediately turn right at the next fork.

You will descend to a private yard nearby on MA 20. Veer left on the trail, stay-ing in the woods, until the trail reverses direction and climbs. Veer right at the next fork and you will arrive back at Stage Road. Turn right and ride back to the intersection with Dearth Hill Road. Turn right and ride back to the parking lot.

RIDE 12 *BIRCH HILL WILDLIFE MANAGEMENT AREA*

According to local mountain bikers, the secluded yet well-maintained Birch Hill area has over 100 miles of old dirt roads and trails. This easy-to-moderate nine-mile ride links three loops: two circuits on grassy single-track trails through fields, and a longer loop on double-track trails in the woods. All three loops happen to run along rivers. They're connected by a mile or so of two-wheel-drive dirt roads.

The area is known locally by three different names: Birch Hill Wildlife Management Area, Lake Denison, and Otter River State Forest. No matter what you call it, it's a well-kept secret in central Massachusetts, and is laced with old dirt roads and trails that are great for mountain biking. You can head west and north of this ride for hillier terrain. There's also swimming and camping at the scenic, popular Denison Lake.

General location: This area lies just north of Winchendon, off MA 2.

Elevation change: The ride is quite flat, with only occasional short climbs and descents.

Season: You can ride here in all 4 seasons, but expect some mud in the spring.

Services: All services are available in Gardner and Fitchburg, including O'Neil's Bicycle Shop on Main Street in Gardner, (508) 632-7200.

Hazards: Watch out for occasional groups of horseback riders and occasional motorized vehicles on the dirt roads. Also, wear brightly colored clothing during hunting season, which lasts from around late October through December.

Rescue index: At most you will be about 1 mile from help.

Land status: Public trails and roads on public land.

Maps: USGS, 7.5 minute series, Winchendon, MA-NH. John's Sport Shop on Main Street in Gardner, (508) 632-0620, stocks maps of this and other mountain biking areas in central Massachusetts.

Finding the trail: From MA 2 in Gardner, take MA 68 toward Baldwinville. Turn right on US 202 North in Baldwinville. After about 1.5 miles you will pass a large brown sign for Otter River State Forest. Go past that sign, and turn left at a second brown sign: "Lake Denison Recreational Area." At a brown gate on the right for Birch Hill Dam, fork left through an open gate. Then veer right and you will reach the parking area at Lake Denison. You can pay and park at the lake, or continue along the paved road around the bend. Park at the turnoffs.

Sources of additional information:

> Department of Environmental Management
> Division of Forests and Parks
> 100 Cambridge Street

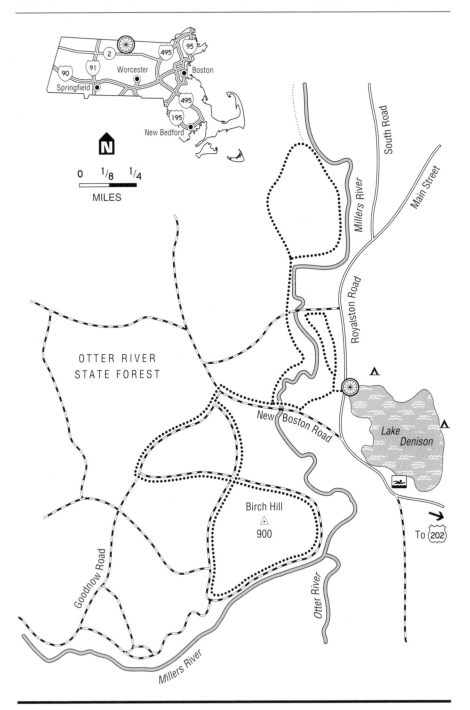

Not all rocks can be hopped. Winchendon, Massachusetts.

Boston, MA 02202
(617) 727-3180
Ask for information about Otter River State Forest.

Notes on the trail: This ride is comprised of 3 loops joined by a two-wheel-drive dirt road, New Boston Road.

Loop 1: Ride clockwise around the lake on the paved road until you reach the Lake Denison boat launching ramp on the right. Just across from it, turn left onto a single-track trail. Bear right and pick up a wider trail paralleling paved Royalston Road (which is on the right). At a junction with a trail on the left, continue straight on a grassier trail to do a counterclockwise loop. You will reach a wide dirt road. Turn left on it, and when you see the river on the right, fork left into the woods. You are now doubling back. When you reach a wider trail again turn right, and you'll soon reach unpaved New Boston Road at a gate.

Loop 2: Turn right on unpaved New Boston Road, cross a bridge, and after a few hundred feet turn right onto a grassy trail at a gate. Ride through a clearing and next to the river (which is on the right). Stay on the trail next to the river until you reach a fork (about 1.5 miles from New Boston Road).

Continue straight, now heading away from the river. (You can also turn right here and ride farther along the river, returning on US 202.) When you reach a narrow dirt road, turn left. Then fork right and return to New Boston Road on the same trail you came on.

Loop 3: Turn right on New Boston Road, and left at the junction with unpaved Goodnow Road. Almost immediately turn left onto a double-track trail and cross a brook on a concrete bridge. At a 4-way unpaved intersection, fork left onto the narrow Swamp River Road. You will begin riding next to Millers River (which is on the left).

After another half mile or so, fork right. (The left fork will take you to Birch Hill Dam.) After another half mile or so, turn left at the same 4-way intersection you approached from the other direction. You will reach a gate at the unpaved Goodnow Road. Turn right and rejoin New Boston Road, and turn right again to reach Lake Denison. (You can turn left on Goodnow Road or left on New Boston Road to explore more old roads and trails.)

RIDE 13 *LAKE DENISON AREA*

This easy 8.5-mile loop ride explores both uninhabited and inhabited countryside, using scenic old roads. About five miles of the ride are on two-wheel-drive and four-wheel-drive dirt roads, while another three miles or so use patchy old asphalt roads. At times you'll feel like you're in Vermont or Maine, cruising through a secluded landscape of grassy fields, light woods, and wetlands along a river. Beginning at the popular, tree-lined Lake Denison, you head out on a narrow, hard-packed road, with some rugged sections and loose gravel. Next, you pass through inhabited countryside, before reentering the Birch Hill Wildlife Management Area on a shady road bordered by a stone wall.

According to local mountain bikers, this area has over 100 miles of old dirt roads and trails. This ride can be linked with the Birch Hill Wildlife Management Area ride.

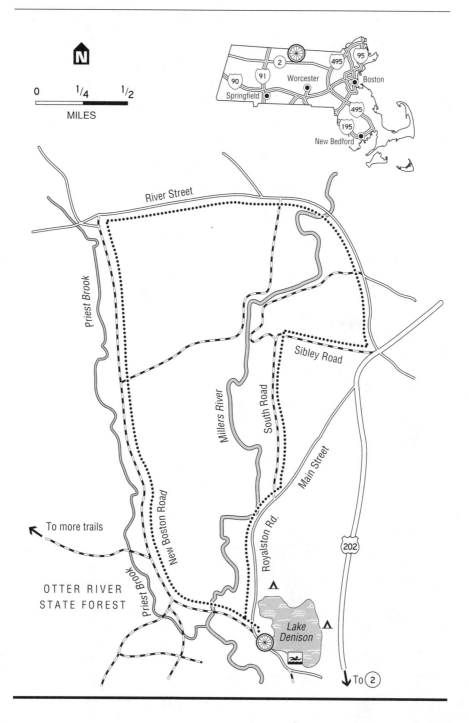

Cruising through a pastoral landscape. Winchendon, Massachusetts.

General location: The area is just north of Winchendon and MA 2.

Elevation change: The terrain is relatively flat, with occasional short climbs and descents.

Season: This is a 4-season ride, so expect some mud in the spring.

Services: All services are available in Fitchburg and Gardner, including O'Neil's Bicycle Shop on Main Street in Gardner, (508) 632-7200. There is camping at Lake Denison.

Hazards: None, except for occasional motorized vehicles on the roads.

Rescue index: You are riding on active roads.

Land status: Town roads.

Maps: USGS, 7.5 minute series, Winchendon, MA-NH. John's Sport Shop on Main Street in Gardner, (508) 632-0620, stocks maps of this area, as well as other mountain biking sites in central Massachusetts.

Finding the trail: From MA 2 in Gardner, take MA 68 toward Baldwinville. Turn right on MA 202 North in Baldwinville. After about 1.5 miles you will pass a large brown sign for Otter River State Forest. Go past that sign, and turn left at a second brown sign: "Lake Denison Recreational Area." At a brown gate on the right for Birch Hill Dam, fork left through an open gate. Then veer right and you will reach the parking area at Lake Denison. You can pay and park at the lake, or continue along the paved road, around the bend, and park at turnoffs.

Sources of additional information:

Department of Environmental Management
Division of Forests and Parks
100 Cambridge Street
Boston, MA 02202
(617) 727-3180

Notes on the trail: Head north from Lake Denison on unpaved New Boston Road. (You will pass dirt roads heading off into the woods—more riding possibilities.) After 3 miles you come out at a T junction on a paved road at the border of Winchendon and Royalston. Turn right. Fork right at the next major intersection, after about 2 miles, and you will reach a stop sign on paved MA 202. Turn right, and immediately right again onto Sibley Road. At the next fork turn left, heading south. You will pass a sign announcing the Birch Hill Wildlife Management Area. When you reach an intersection, turn right onto paved Royalston Road. (Again, dirt roads you might want to explore will appear on the right.) Lake Denison comes up on the left.

RIDE 14   *LEOMINSTER STATE FOREST*

This moderate seven-mile ride connects four rugged woods roads into a loop through quiet, scenic woods. These abandoned dirt roads are often no wider than a double-track trail, with plenty of exposed bedrock, eroded areas, loose terrain, and an occasional shallow waterhole. The habitat is varied and handsome: a mix of hardwoods and softwoods, mountain laurel bushes, low-level ferns and mosses, and boulders strewn here and there. In places, the forest looks like a New England version of a classic Japanese garden. This popular mountain biking area also has a swimming beach and many picnic areas at the trailhead.

General location: The forest is located on MA 31, just south of Fitchburg, and 40 miles west of Boston.
Elevation change: You will climb gently from 750' to 950', then descend to about 700', and climb back to 950', for a total elevation gain of 450'.
Season: Summer and fall are best for riding here, but this can be a 4-season ride if there has been little snow and not too much wetness in the spring.
Services: All services are available in Fitchburg and Gardner, including O'Neil's Bicycle Shop on Main Street in Gardner, (508) 632-7200.
Hazards: None.

RIDE 14 *LEOMINSTER STATE FOREST*

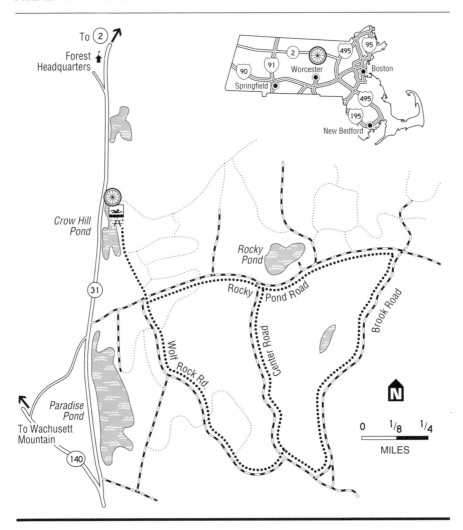

Rescue index: At most you will be about 1 mile from a traveled road.

Land status: Abandoned roads and active trails in a state forest.

Maps: Pick up a map at the forest headquarters, (508) 874-2303, on MA 31 near the trailhead, or contact the Department of Environmental Management (see below).

Finding the trail: On MA 2 take the Fitchburg/Princeton Exit onto MA 31 South. After 1 mile, you will pass the forest headquarters on the right, and then a pond (Crow Hill Pond) on the right. Turn left just before the pond and park in

Heading into a forest. Leominster State Forest, Leominster, Massachusetts.

a large parking lot. If the gate is closed (in the off-season), park at turnoffs near the gate along MA 31.

Sources of additional information:

Leominster State Forest
Route 31
Princeton, MA 01541
(508) 874-2303

Department of Environmental Management
Division of Forests and Parks
100 Cambridge Street
Boston, MA 02202
(617) 727-3180

Notes on the trail: Pick up a double-track trail along the near (eastern) shore of Crow Hill Pond, and head south following blue blazes. After about a half mile on this flat trail, you will reach wide Rocky Pond Road (which becomes much narrower as it goes deeper into the woods). Straight ahead is Wolf Rock Road, one of the two woods roads on which you can return.

Turn left onto Rocky Pond Road. After about a mile, you will pass Center

Road on the right (where this loop will come out). Continue straight and you will pass Rocky Pond on the left, with a side trail down to it. After climbing again, turn right at a distinct intersection with Brook Road.

Stay to the right at the next fork, descend, and you will reach Center Road. Turn right and you'll soon reach a fork. Now you can take the left fork uphill onto Wolf Rock Road, or the right turn onto Center Road. Either road comes out on Rocky Pond Road. Then turn left and return to the trailhead.

This forest also has many miles of winding single-track trails (created by off-road motorcyclists). Many of them are found off Rocky Pond Road. Informal mountain bike rides congregate in the parking lot on weekends.

RIDE 15 *DOUGLAS STATE FOREST*

This moderate 12-mile ride combines both loops and out-and-back stretches as it crosses a 4,500-acre forest. About half of the 30-plus miles of trails in the forest are loose-gravel and dirt roads built during the Depression by the Civilian Conservation Corps. This massive public works project employed thousands of citizens, who built hundreds of miles of roads and trails in parks and forests throughout Massachusetts. Mountain bikers are now benefiting from these federal projects. The rest of the routes in this forest are double- and single-track trails—some grassy, others covered with lots of rocks. Finally, a rail-trail—once the New Haven & Hartford Railroad line, but now a flat, wide cinder path—intersects the forest, extending for miles in either direction.

In the deeper woods, you will find oak, ash, and pine trees alternating with wetlands and grassy clearings. In many places, the ground is also strewn with granite boulders and supports the occasional rare wild orchid. Along the trails you'll pass blueberries (ripe in late summer), small wintergreen plants (they stay green all winter and smell like wintergreen chewing gum when broken open), and tall flowering rhododendron bushes in the southern part of the forest.

At the southern trailhead, there's popular Wallum Lake, with a beach, boating, lawns, and shaded picnic areas. At the northern end of the forest, at an old mill site by Wallis Pond, a stream still tumbles over a dam.

General location: The forest is in Douglas, which is in the corner of Massachusetts, Connecticut, and Rhode Island.
Elevation change: The terrain is relatively flat, with a few climbs and descents on loose-gravel roads.
Season: Any time between mid-May and late fall is good for riding here; expect some mosquitoes in the spring. Autumn offers spectacular foliage colors.
Services: Wallum Lake has water fountains, water spigots, and restrooms. All

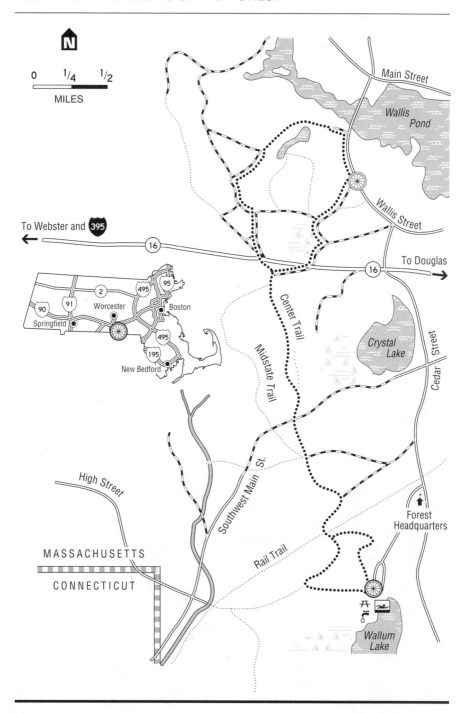

other services are available in Douglas. Bicycles Plus bike shop is located north of the ride on MA 146 in Sutton, (508) 865-5229.

Hazards: Stay alert for changing riding conditions, from hard-packed dirt to loose-gravel, to steep tricky sections on some of the narrower trails. Yield to the riders on horseback you'll see occasionally.

Rescue index: At most you will be about 1 mile from a well-traveled road.

Land status: State forest roads and trails.

Maps: There is a trail map on a board at Wallum Lake near the trailhead. For your own copy, contact the Department of Environmental Management (see below).

Finding the trail: Take MA 16 through Douglas and, several miles west of the town, watch for brown signs for the state forest. Turn left at a forest sign at Cedar Street and follow signs for the forest. Another trailhead comes up if you turn right on Cedar Street; turn off soon onto Wallis Street. This is a good place to begin gentler loops around Wallis Pond and Wallis Reservoir.

Sources of additional information:

Douglas State Forest
Wallum Lake Road
Douglas, MA 01516
(508) 476-7872

Department of Environmental Management
Division of Forests and Parks
100 Cambridge Street
Boston, MA 02202
(617) 727-3180

Notes on the trail: You can explore many different trails in this elongated area. Our ride travels from south to north, using a half-dozen or so trails. From the picnic area at Wallum Lake, ride north up a smooth, sandy road behind the bathhouse, passing a cabin on the right. Soon you will pass a sign for the Cedar Swamp Trail. This is a popular single-track hiking loop. (Stay off it on busy weekends.)

At the next junction, fork left onto a narrower double-track trail. Then turn right on a trail marked "Coffee House Loop." This is also a hiking trail. It will become a steep, rocky single-track trail for a while. Cross a wooden bridge and go straight on a wider trail at a fork, where the Coffee House Loop turns right. Almost immediately, you will intersect the rail-trail, a sunny, flat, wide, loose-gravel path that you can pedal in either direction.

Ride across the rail-trail and follow the yellow blazes, which mark the Midstate Trail, an 85-mile north-south hiking trail through the center of Massachusetts. (In about a half mile you will keep going straight, getting off the Midstate Trail, which becomes almost impassable north of Southwest Main Street).

After crossing the rail-trail, you must maneuver around a couple of large, deep

A double-track trail. Douglas State Forest, Douglas, Massachusetts.

mudholes. Afterward, fork right and then left at an intersection of 4 gravel roads, and left again at a fork with another gravel road. Then go straight across a 4-way intersection of gravel roads (the Midstate Trail heads left).

You will reach gravel Southwest Main Street at a gate. Pick up a single-track trail on the other side of the road, and soon veer left on a wider trail, still heading north. This is the Center Trail, which is dotted with rocks. At 4 miles you come out at a T junction. Turn left and reach paved MA 16. On the other side of MA 16 pick up another woods road, and soon turn left on a dirt and gravel road.

At the next fork, you can go straight for a longer ride, or turn right to reach the mill site on Wallis Pond. Turn right and, after cruising on a grassy trail, you will cross the bridge at the mill site and pick up a dirt road on the left that meets paved Wallis Street. (You can also keep going straight just before the mill site for a scenic ride along Wallis Pond and up a hill.)

Turn right on paved Wallis Street; you'll soon reach a parking area and a large brown gate. Turn right onto a gravel road heading into the forest. Take the second left fork onto a narrower double-track trail and then turn right at a T junction with 3 red blazes on a tree. You will come out at MA 16. Turn right and pick up a dirt road on the left. Then fork left on the same trail that you rode up. From here, you can retrace your route back to Wallis Lake, or explore some other woods roads. Again, the Midstate Trail just to the west of Center Trail is extremely difficult.

RIDE 16 *UPTON STATE FOREST*

This moderate 5.5-mile loop ride combines easy going on wide, flat double-track trails with more challenging riding on single-track trails and climbs on loose-gravel roads. You will also cross both a rideable pipeline trail and a rideable power line trail, as well as several other woods roads and trails.

Like many mountain biking sites in New England, this one is a mixed wood-scape of tall pine trees, shorter hardwoods and evergreens, a mid-level canopy of bushes, and low-lying groundcover. About a mile into the ride there's also a giant old apple tree hugging the trail, which still bears edible fruit in summer.

Later in the ride, you will maneuver around a small pond on a single-track trail and come out at a stone dam. Finally, at the height-of-land on a gravel road, a trail forks off to a scenic overlook.

General location: This forest is located 5 miles west of Interstate 495, 30 miles west of Boston, and 30 miles north of Providence, Rhode Island.

Elevation change: The ride begins with a steady, gradual descent for 1.5 miles. On its backside, there's a moderately steep climb for a half mile. The rest of the ride is flat or gently rolling.

Season: This is a 4-season ride, with some muddy areas in the spring, colorful foliage in the fall, and snowmobile-packed trails in the winter. Mountain biking in shallow snow can be fun, but not if it's icy.

Services: All services are available in Milford to the south, including Milford Bicycle on Main Street, a full-service bike shop with information about mountain biking in the area. There is no drinking water available in the forest.

Hazards: Be prepared to change riding techniques when switching from flatter, smoother trails to technical climbs and descents over loose rock and minor obstructions. Also, watch for occasional motorized off-road vehicles.

Rescue index: At most you will be about 1 mile from a traveled road.

RIDE 16 *UPTON STATE FOREST*

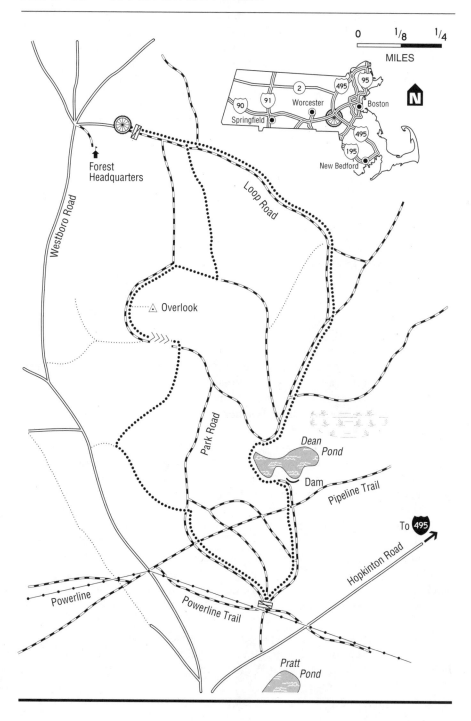

Land status: Public roads and trails in a state forest.

Maps: The Department of Environmental Management (DEM) provides free maps of most state forests and parks in Massachusetts (see below).

Finding the trail: Take Exit 21B on Interstate 495 and head west toward Upton on MA 135. After about 3.5 miles, turn sharply right at a large pond on the left (Pratt Pond), onto Westboro Road. After 1.9 miles, follow brown signs to the left for the state forest, and immediately take the right-hand dirt road for a short distance to an unpaved parking area. Lock your vehicle.

Sources of additional information:

Milford Bicycle
71 East Main Street
Milford, MA 01757
(508) 473-7955

Department of Environmental Management
Division of Forests and Parks
100 Cambridge Street
Boston, MA 02202
(617) 727-3180

Notes on the trail: Head through the gate, onto a wide jeep trail (Loop Road). Follow the trail steadily downhill until you reach Dean Pond (after 1.7 miles). Turn right, and then left into the second small cove along the pond. In this cove, turn right onto a single-track trail that skirts the pond counterclockwise. Keep following this short single-track trail around the shoreline. Then cross a small dam, then another dam. You'll come out on a wider jeep trail (Gore Road).

Turn right (south), and after a few hundred feet you will cross the Pipeline Trail. This trail is rideable in either direction, although it is more challenging than the woods roads and has several wide mudholes along it. Continue on Gore Road until you reach a gate at the forest's southern border. (Or, just after the Pipeline Trail, turn right onto another double-track trail, left at a T junction onto another trail, and reach the same southern boundary.) Ride up to the gate and check out an intersecting trail along a powerline, which stretches for miles in either direction. Like the Pipeline Trail, it is rideable but more challenging than the forest trails.

Now ride back northward, forking almost immediately onto the left-most trail. You will cross the Pipeline Trail again. Soon afterward, look for a double-track trail on the left. Turn onto it and climb. After about a half mile, turn sharply right onto another double-track trail. (If you miss it, you will soon reach paved Westboro Road.)

This trail comes out onto the gravelly Park Road. Turn left on the road and climb. At the height-of-land, look for a gravel parking area on the right with an overgrown single-track trail off it. You can take this short side trail to a scenic overlook.

While going downhill on Park Road, turn right onto a single-track trail. (You can also stay on Park Road and take it to Loop Road.) After descending on this single-track trail for a short distance, turn left at the next intersection, onto another trail, and you will intersect dirt Loop Road. Turn left on it and return to the parking area.

RIDE 17 *AYER-PEPPERELL LINE*

This former railroad bed is now an 8.5-mile cinder path running through three quaint towns in central Massachusetts. Its southern half has some loose sand and gravel, which creates a bit of pedaling resistance, and a section of rollercoaster-like berms made by motorized dirt bikes. The northern half of the ride is smoother and more hard-packed. You can take a 17-mile out-and-back ride on the trail, or loop through scenic New England countryside on paved MA 111.

The trail quickly leaves civilization, passing through an uninhabited landscape of light woods and fields, with an occasional house visible. Between Ayer and Groton, the trail runs a short distance along a secluded body of water, where you might see geese. At its Pepperell end, it borders a 500-acre state forest with a large pond and tall pine trees lining the path. (The state forest has a network of trails that intersect the rail-trail.) An extra feature is two short tunnels.

General location: This former railroad line runs due north through the towns of Ayer, Groton, and Pepperell, and continues into New Hampshire.
Elevation change: Flat. Railroad beds were never inclined more than 2 degrees.
Season: The ride can be done in all 4 seasons. Cool and colorful fall is the best season. Expect some wetness and occasional mosquitoes in the spring.
Services: All services are available just off the trail in Ayer, Groton, and Pepperell. A block off the trail in Groton are a bakery, pharmacy, and other stores, as well as some grand homes.
Hazards: Be sure to scan for traffic at all cross streets; motorists are not always expecting cyclists to come out of the woods. Also, watch out for occasional loose terrain, an eroded shoulder, and an occasional minor obstruction (like a tree branch).
Rescue index: At most you will be about a half mile from a traveled road.
Land status: This former railroad bed is now a public right-of-way.
Maps: Any detailed state road map will show the access roads.
Finding the trail: You can begin in either Ayer, Pepperell, or at the midpoint in Groton. From the south, on MA 2, take the exit for MA 110 and MA 111/Ayer/Groton. After 1.8 miles, follow signs around the rotary for Ayer. After another 2.5 miles, you will reach downtown Ayer. At Main Street and Park Street, pick up the trail behind a parking lot. In Groton, the trail lies 1 block off MA 119 on

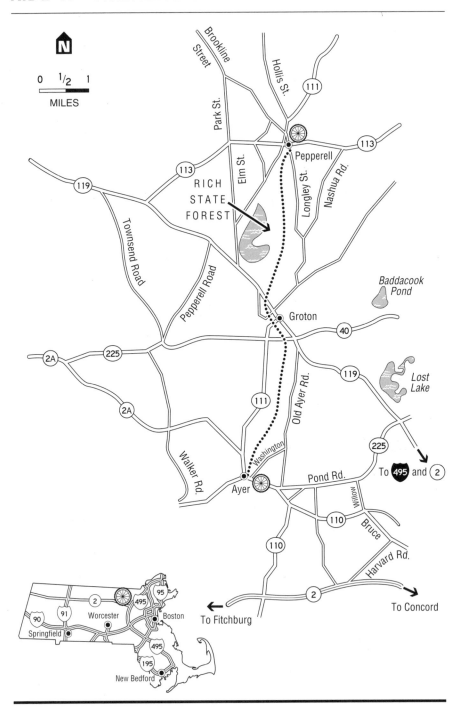

A tunnel on a rail-trail. Ayer, Massachusetts.

Court Street, just south of the junction of MA 111 and MA 119. In Pepperell, the trail crosses the junction of MA 113 and Longley Street in East Pepperell, just opposite a row of stores and a gas station (with an air hose).

Sources of additional information:

Rails-to-Trails Conservancy
1400 16th Street, N.W.
Washington, DC 20036
(202) 797-5400
Hundreds of miles of railroad tracks in the U.S. are abandoned each year. The Rails-to-Trails Conservancy helps to convert these public corridors into multi-use trails—before they revert to private ownership. Annual

membership fees are small, but do much to assure additional trails for cyclists.

Notes on the trail: The trail from Pepperell southward is smoother, with fewer berms and mudholes. At the halfway point lies Groton, a handsome, well-to-do community. If you prefer a loop ride, take MA 111, a scenic rural highway that is almost entirely downhill from Groton to Ayer. You can pick it up off Main Street in Groton.

Eastern Massachusetts

RIDE 18 LOWELL-DRACUT-TYNGSBORO STATE PARK

This moderate eight-mile loop ride twists and turns through a 1,000-acre forest on a compact network of single- and double-track trails and woods roads. You can do some challenging and fast riding on these rugged trails and old roads that wind past wetlands, deep woods, and huge granite outcroppings.

You will also ride on two connecting paved stretches through rural-suburban countryside. In the middle of the ride, there's a loop through a wooded area used by Native Americans for powwows—singing and dancing, craftmaking, and food gatherings. These are held in the summer and fall throughout New England, and are usually open to the public.

General location: This forest is located just north of Lowell, off MA 113, 30 miles north of Boston.

Elevation change: The terrain is relatively flat.

Season: Any time between late spring and late fall is good for riding here. Expect plenty of mud in the spring.

Services: All services are available in Lowell, Dracut, and Tyngsboro, and along MA 113.

Hazards: Yield to occasional horseback riders. Also, because this area is near a city (Lowell), watch out for occasional litter.

Rescue index: At most you will be about a half mile from well-traveled roads.

Land status: State park roads and trails.

Maps: Call or write the Department of Environmental Management for a free map (see below).

Finding the trail: From MA 3, take Exit 34 onto MA 113 East toward Tyngsboro. After a mile, you will reach MA 3A and a large bridge across the Merrimack River. Cross the bridge and fork immediately right. After 3.3 miles, just past a contemporary-looking church on the left, turn left onto Trotting Park Road. After three-tenths of a mile, you will begin to see large iron gates at trailheads on the right. This ride begins behind the first gate, behind an abandoned field house. There is parking at turnoffs or in a parking lot a short distance farther up Trotting Park Road.

Sources of additional information:

Lowell-Dracut-Tyngsboro State Park
Trotting Park Road

RIDE 18 *LOWELL-DRACUT-TYNGSBORO STATE FOREST*

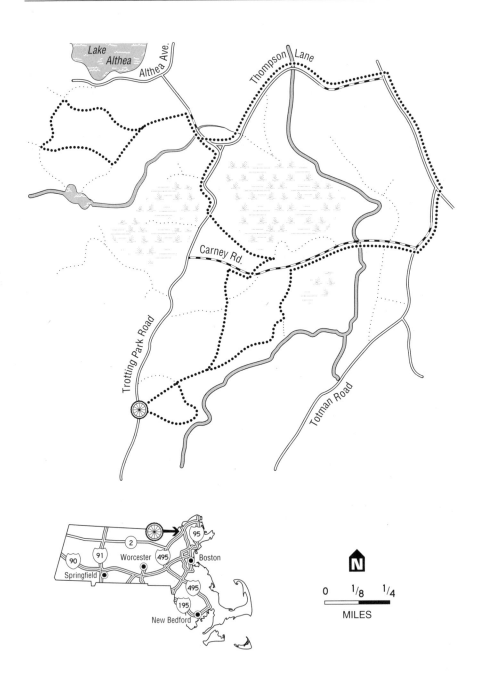

An active Native American powwow site. Lowell-Dracut-Tyngsboro State Park, Lowell, Massachusetts.

Lowell, MA 01853
(508) 453-1950

Department of Environmental Management
Division of Forests and Parks
100 Cambridge Street
Boston, MA 02202
(617) 727-3180

Notes on the trail: This loop ride uses many of the trails and woods roads in this compact area. Although it has quite a few turns on it, it's not really all that complicated. Any trail you take, even a "wrong" one, will soon intersect one of three woods roads, or else reach a paved road.

Take the single-track trail to the left behind the abandoned field house. Turn right at the next fork and, after just another one-tenth of a mile, go straight uphill at an intersection. Then fork left onto a wider trail with blue markers on it, and then turn left again.

You will come out on a dirt woods road, Carney Road. Turn right on it, and almost immediately turn left onto a single-track trail. Shortly, just before riding into a swamp, fork left and skirt the wetland area on another single-track trail.

You will reach a narrow paved woods road, Trotting Park Road. Turn right on it. (There are short double-track dead-end trails you can explore on either side of this road.)

At a 3-way intersection of roads, fork left and reach a gate and an unpaved gravel road leaving the park. Just past a home, there is a gate on the left at a dirt road; a sign says, "Historic Pawtucket Indian Site/Greater Lowell Indian Cultural Association." (This sign also asks users to be considerate of this Native American land.) Ride up this dirt road, fork left, and turn right into the woods on a double-track trail.

At a T junction, turn right onto a wider path, and then fork right again. You will reach the same woods roads on which you entered this part of the forest. Turn left, backtrack to the paved road, and turn right to return to the three-way intersection just inside the main forest.

Now fork left and follow this paved woods road until it leaves the park, becomes a rugged jeep road, passes behind several homes, and comes out at a rural highway. Turn right on the pavement, ride past a farm, and fork right onto Totman Road. The road becomes unpaved at another park gate. Fork right onto unpaved Carney Road, and then watch for a left turn onto a double-track trail. Take this trail, heading south, and just before reaching a wetlands clearing turn right, uphill, onto a single-track trail.

At a T junction, turn left downhill, fork right, and at another T junction turn left. Go through an intersection and you will be back at the trailhead. (At the last intersection you can turn right to take another trail back to Trotting Park Road.)

RIDE 19 *GREAT BROOK FARM STATE PARK*

This is the place to bring someone you want to introduce to the sport of mountain biking. Created around a working dairy farm, this 935-acre park has 20 miles or so of scenic trails through open fields, woods, and wetlands. You're never far from a trailhead, and there's an ice-cream stand for post-ride treats. The countryside looks like it could be in southern Vermont, with well-maintained farms and an occasional pond harboring geese.

The moderate ten-mile ride that I suggest also takes you past wetlands where peeper frogs call insistently in the spring. (You can orient yourself by their sound.) Along the Woodchuck Trail (to the east) you will cruise through hundreds of bright green pine saplings under cathedral-like white pines. This tallest indigenous New England tree once dominated the landscape, but that was before European settlers discovered how valuable it was for a host of uses, including ship masts.

The main trails here are pine-covered and grassy double-track. More challenging single-track trails branch off them, and a wide, rugged gas pipeline trail

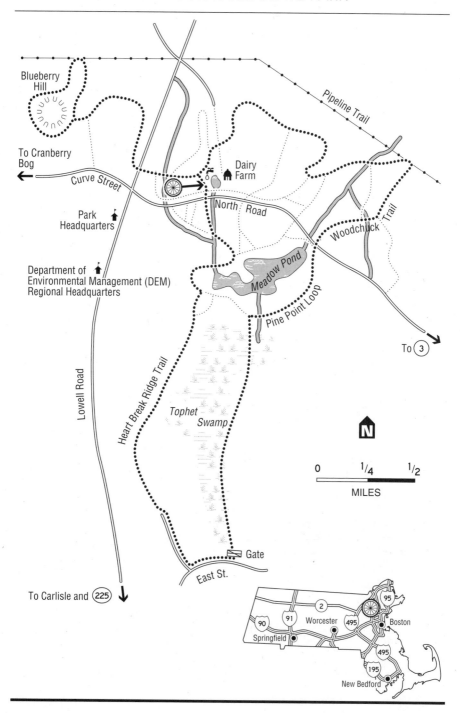

Blueberry
Hill

To Cranberry
Bog

Curve Street

Pipeline Trail

Dairy
Farm

North Road

Woodchuck Trail

Park
Headquarters

Department of
Environmental Management (DEM)
Regional Headquarters

Meadow Pond

Pine Point Loop

To ③

Lowell Road

Heart Break Ridge Trail

Tophet
Swamp

N

0   ¼   ½
MILES

Gate

East St.

To Carlisle and ㉕

95

2

Worcester

495

Boston

90   91

Springfield

495

195

New Bedford

runs along the northern border of the park. You can also relax around the scenic pond at the dairy farm. A short ride across paved Lowell Road and onto Curve Street to the west, there's a colorful cranberry bog—the northernmost one in Massachusetts—with a trail circumventing it.

General location: In the town of Carlisle, about 12 miles north of Concord.

Elevation change: This area is relatively flat, with some rolling terrain and small hills. Some single-track trails have short, steep ascents, and the pipeline to the north has longer climbs and descents.

Season: Any time between spring and fall is good for riding here, though some of the trails are muddy in the spring. Winter is usually reserved for cross-country skiers, if there's enough snow on the ground.

Services: There are portable restrooms, a farm stand, and water at the trailhead. All other services are available in the nearby towns of Chelmsford, Bedford, and Concord. Lincoln Guide Service, a bike shop in Lincoln (about 10 miles south of the ride), has a lot of maps and information on mountain biking in the region. It also rents mountain bikes and sponsors group rides. Phone: (617) 259-9204.

Hazards: Watch for hikers and horseback riders, especially around the trail-heads and ponds. Also, the trail around Tophet Swamp (to the south) and the pipeline trail (to the north) have a few minor obstructions—although one rider's hazard is another rider's hop.

Rescue index: You will be no more than a half mile from paved roads and homes.

Land status: State park trails.

Maps: Maps are usually stocked in a box at the parking lot. Otherwise, contact the Department of Environmental Management (see below).

Finding the trail: From the south, take Lowell Road out of Concord, heading north toward Carlisle. Pass through the center of Carlisle and veer left toward Chelmsford. After about 1.5 miles, you will pass a regional headquarters for the Department of Environmental Management (DEM) on the left. (The DEM manages most parks and forests in Massachusetts.) Turn right soon after the headquarters at a sign for the park. After one-third of a mile you will reach the parking lot on the left.

Sources of additional information:

Great Brook Farm State Park
841 Lowell Street
Carlisle, MA 01741
(508) 369-6312

Department of Environmental Management
Division of Forests and Parks
100 Cambridge Street
Boston, MA 02202
(617) 727-3180

Riding across a corn field. Great Brook Farm State Park, Carlisle, Massachusetts.

Notes on the trail: Fanning out from the pond and farm at the parking area are trails heading into different areas. This ride links up most of these riding spots. To take a 2.5-mile loop around Tophet Swamp to the south, cross North Road from the parking lot and pick up a double-track trail with a blue sign on it. At a **T** junction, turn left and you will reach the Pine Point Loop. Turn left for a short loop. Otherwise, turn right, cross a small bridge, pass a field on the right and, after going downhill, turn up a single-track trail on the right. This is Heart Break Ridge Trail, which becomes a pine needle-covered single-track.

After about 1.5 miles, you will come out at a paved road, Woodbine Road, which continues heading south. Turn left at the **T** junction with East Street. Look for a left turn back into the woods at a metal gate. On the way north, you must deal with 2 or 3 short swampy areas, which you can walk around.

Keep going north on this rugged trail until you reach an intersection with the smoother, wider Pine Point Loop Trail, which has large blue diamond markings on it. Turn right and come out on North Road, near a small dam on Meadow Pond and a parking lot.

Across the road you can pick up a wide double-track trail, Woodchuck Trail. On it, you will pass an old mill site, log house, stone bridge, stone walls, and giant pine trees. Now you can try short loops to the southeast, continue north to link up with the pipeline trail, or veer left and reach several loops heading back toward the trailhead through fields near the cow barn.

Just west of this ride, across Lowell Road, a trail on the right side of the road goes along more fields to reach Blueberry Hill. From Blueberry Hill, you can pick up the pipeline to the north, head west on it, reach Martin Street, turn left on it, and pick up trails on the right heading toward the cranberry bog.

RIDE 20 *HAROLD PARKER STATE FOREST*

This second-oldest state park in Massachusetts has plenty of riding opportunities on its approximately 25 miles of trails and jeep roads. The woods roads through this 3,000-acre area wind around a half-dozen ponds, while double- and single-track trails cut through woods and grassy wetlands, passing granite outcroppings and pine-lined ponds. Depending on whether you stay on the woods roads or tackle the trails, a ride can be anywhere from easy to difficult. This moderate ten-mile loop alternates between trails and roads.

The forest is convenient to many cities and towns in northeastern Massachusetts, including Lowell, Lawrence, Haverhill, Reading, Burlington, and Lynn. It has many campsites (providing that the state budget is not cut further) and a swimming beach on Stearns Pond (also threatened by budget cuts).

General location: The forest is in Andover and North Andover, 25 miles north of Boston.

Elevation change: The terrain is relatively flat, with some rolling sections and short climbs.

Season: Plenty of shade and ponds make this a good summer ride. There is some mud in the spring and, if there's snow in the winter, some trails are used by cross-country skiers. Autumn brings colorful foliage.

Services: All services are available in Andover and North Reading, including The Cycle Shop on MA 62 in North Reading, (508) 664-6420. The state forest also offers campsites.

Hazards: Watch for walkers, horseback riders, and other trail users, especially around the ponds and trailheads. The terrain sometimes changes abruptly from wide, flat woods roads to narrow, winding trails, and you will cross several paved roads.

Rescue index: You are always close to well-traveled roads and homes.

Land status: State park roads and trails.

Maps: Maps are usually stocked in a box outside park headquarters. Or you can contact the Department of Environmental Management (see below).

Finding the trail: Take Exit 41 off Interstate 93 and turn right onto MA 125 North toward Andover. After 2.5 miles, just after the state police barracks, turn right toward a sign for the state forest. You will pass between 2 large stone pillars onto Harold Parker Road. Follow signs for forest headquarters (where trail maps

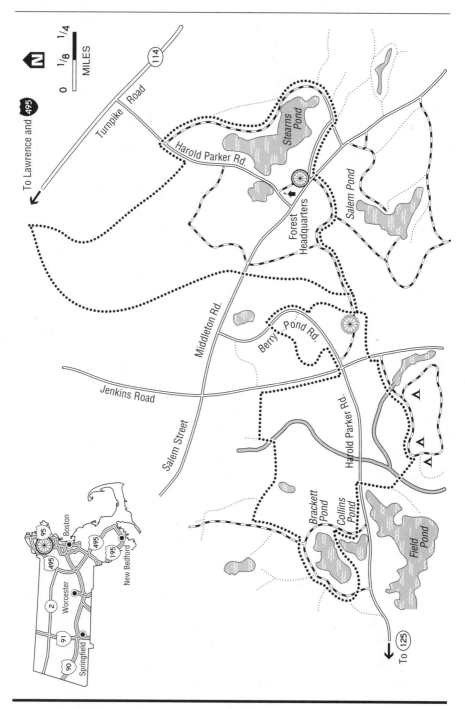

Circumventing a pond. Harold Parker State Forest, Andover, Massachusetts.

are stocked). Along the way, you can also park at turnoffs at several trailheads along Harold Parker Road, near several ponds. There's another large parking area just beyond the intersection of Harold Parker Road and Jenkins Road.

Sources of additional information:

Harold Parker State Forest
1951 North Turnpike Road
North Andover, MA 01845
(508) 686-3391

Department of Environmental Management
Division of Forests and Parks
100 Cambridge Street
Boston, MA 02202
(617) 727-3180

Notes on the trail: In each of the 4 sections of this spread-out forest there are loops and networks of trails and woods roads that can be connected using paved roads. (Some of the woods roads have short trails branching off them that dead-end at private property. If you take one, just double back and pick up the main trail.)

Shorter loops: The flat double-track trails around Brackett Pond and Collins Pond in the western part of the forest are easy and scenic. A longer, more challenging trail runs for 3 miles into the northern part of the forest between Middleton Road and Turnpike Road. The shorter woods road loop inside it is another possible loop. A compact network of single-track trails laces the hills just north of Berry Pond Road.

A long loop: Begin riding on a jeep road heading southwest, just across from forest headquarters. Turn right at a fork, and then left at the next one. You will reach a large gravel parking area (another possible trailhead). Take a sharp left turn out of the gravel lot onto a single-track trail and reach paved Jenkins Road. Turn left for a few hundred feet on the road and then right onto a paved access road into the camping area.

Stay to the right on the access road (watching out for walkers) and, at the bottom of the camping area, turn right, cross a brook, and turn left immediately onto a single-track trail. Cross a couple of streams and reach a T junction at a double-track trail. Turn right, ride along Field Pond, and come out on Harold Parker Road. Then turn left on the pavement and pick up a double-track trail on the other side of the road. This trail will merge with a wider old road.

You can now circumvent Brackett Pond and Collins Pond, or head north and pick up a trail on the right toward Jenkins Road. Then take single-track trails heading east, a long loop trail northward to Turnpike Road, and finally pick up a woods road around Stearns Pond that leads back to forest headquarters.

RIDE 21 *MAUDSLAY STATE PARK*

This easy six-mile loop ride weaves along the same paths once trodden by famous artists and intellectuals. Maudslay Estate, with its 72-room mansion and formal gardens, was once a popular meeting place for New England luminaries in the late nineteenth and early twentieth centuries. Poets like John Greenleaf Whittier and mystics like Katherine Tingley, founder of the Theosophical Society, gathered here to put on theatrical events and commune with nature.

Today, you can see the remains of the formal gardens (the state is renovating them), as well as hundreds of flowering trees and shrubs, including mountain laurel, rhododendron, azalea, dogwood, crab apple, roses, and dozens of different wildflowers. Also, a two-mile trail runs along the grand Merrimack River,

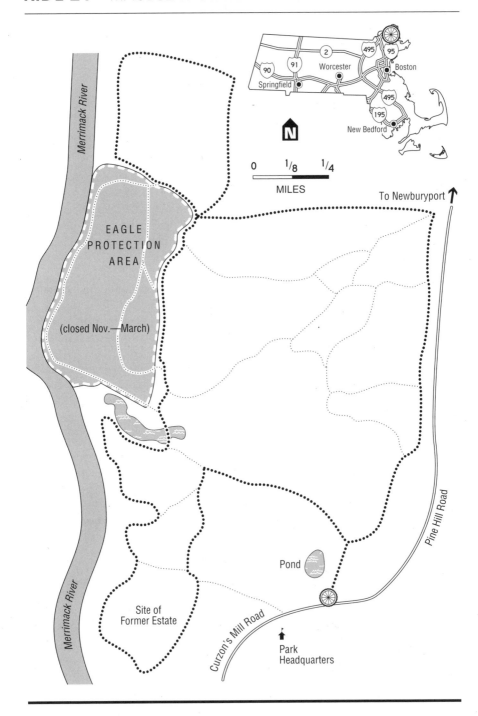

EAGLE
PROTECTION
AREA

(closed Nov.—March)

Merrimack River

To Newburyport

N

0   1/8   1/4

MILES

Worcester
Springfield
90
91
2
495
95
Boston
195
495
New Bedford

Pond

Pine Hill Road

Curzon's Mill Road

Site of
Former Estate

Park
Headquarters

while other trails weave through pine stands and manicured meadows and across stone bridges.

Although these well-maintained trails (called "carriage roads" because they were built for horse-drawn carriages) are easy riding, they're varied, with rolling stretches, sharp turns, and occasional rooted terrain. Needless to say, though, this is not a place to "hammer" through.

A few miles east of Maudslay (named after an ancestral home in England) is Newburyport, once a famous seaport, now a lively coastal town in the summer.

General location: The park is tucked away in Newburyport, 35 miles north of Boston.

Elevation change: The terrain is relatively flat, with regular short climbs and descents.

Season: This is a year-round ride. If you use the trails in the winter, avoid pedaling across cross-country ski tracks.

Services: All services are available in Newburyport.

Hazards: Watch for strollers, especially around blind corners.

Rescue index: At most you will be about a quarter mile from help.

Land status: These are trails in a state park. To avoid accidents and also ensure that biking is always allowed here, be sure to yield to equestrians and avoid surprising walkers from behind.

Maps: Trail maps stocked at the parking area include information about the site's history and flora.

Finding the trail: On Interstate 95 take Exit 57 for Newburyport, and turn right onto MA 113. After four-tenths of a mile, turn left (at a cemetery) onto Noble Street. At the end of the street, turn left onto Ferry Road and follow signs for the park. You will reach a parking area on the left after 1.4 miles.

Sources of additional information:

Maudslay State Park
Curzon's Mill Road
Newburyport, MA 01950
(617) 465-7223

Notes on the trail: Begin riding at a trailhead across from the parking area. To do a perimeter counterclockwise loop, fork right at the trailhead, cutting diagonally across the field (northward). Keep veering right along the boundary of the park. You will reach a 4-way intersection of trails. Take a hard right. Continue riding until you reach the northeast border of the park, turn left, and you will reach the river.

Ride west along this scenic trail. There is also a side trail loop to the right, reached through a low-lying, overgrown area. (From November 1 to March 31 a stretch of land along the river is fenced off. It is one of the few winter nesting areas in the Northeast for bald eagles. A trail skirts the area.)

When you reach the eastern edge of the park, turn south, winding past the estate's formal gardens, and you will reach the trailhead. To extend this ride, head toward the river again on another trail, exploring inner loops.

RIDE 22   *GEORGETOWN-ROWLEY STATE FOREST*

This moderate-to-easy five-mile loop ride in a 1,000-acre forest alternates between single- and double-track trails and jeep roads. The route runs through deep woods past pine and oak trees, wetlands, and, at the northern edge of the forest, an active horse farm. This ride can also be linked with more trails in two adjoining state parks to the southeast, Willowdale and Bradley Palmer.

Throughout these woods you will pass well-preserved stone walls. Local historians are still debating exactly why European settlers built so many stone walls. They do know that many forests like this one were once farmland before settlers discovered fishing and trading and then the rockless Midwest. So they left their farms, which reverted to woods—except for hundreds of miles of the impressive walls of stacked field stones.

General location: This forest spans the towns of Georgetown and Rowley, 30 miles north of Boston.

Elevation change: The terrain is relatively flat, with a few short steep climbs and descents.

Season: Any time between late spring and late fall is good for riding here. Depending on the amount of rainfall, some low-lying trails can be muddy, especially in the spring.

Services: All services are available in Georgetown and other nearby towns, including Two For the Road, a bike shop on Main Street (MA 133) in Georgetown, (508) 352-7343, and Cycle Stop on Union Street in Lawrence, (508) 975-1515.

Hazards: Some of the trails and old roads in this forest are occasionally used by motorized off-road vehicles and horseback riders.

Rescue index: At most you will be about 1 mile from help.

Land status: State forest trails and roads.

Maps: Maps of several local state forests are available at the headquarters of Bradley Palmer State Park on Asbury Street in Topsfield, (508) 887-5931, located 1 mile off MA 1.

Finding the trail: Take Exit 54 off Interstate 95, onto MA 133 West toward Georgetown. At the stoplight in Georgetown, turn left onto MA 97 South. Fork left, staying on MA 97, pass a farm stand on the right and, after just under a mile, pass through an intersection with Elm Street. Turn left onto a narrow paved road (East Street). Bear right on it, fork left toward a sign for the forest, and you will reach the trailhead.

RIDE 22 *GEORGETOWN-ROWLEY STATE FOREST*

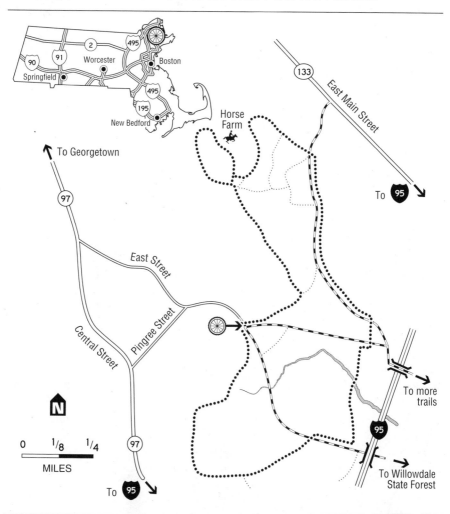

Sources of additional information:

The regional headquarters for three adjoining state parks:
Bradley Palmer State Park
Asbury Street (off MA 1)
Topsfield, MA 01983
(508) 887-5931

Snaking stone walls are the sole remains of former farmland in New England. Georgetown, Massachusetts.

Two for the Road
74 East Main Street (MA 133)
Georgetown, MA 01833
(508) 352-7343

Notes on the trail: About 2 miles into this ride you will reach an area with a network of single-track trails (in the northern part of the forest). At this point, the ride takes a lot of turns. On the ground, though, it's easier to follow. In fact, riding circles in this highly compact area can be half the fun.

From the parking area, take the trail on the right, which goes uphill. (The trail on the left heads east toward a bridge over I-95 and into the eastern half of the forest, with more trails.) Almost immediately, turn right onto a single-track trail that rolls up and down. Veer left and, after about 1 mile, you will reach a T junction with a wider trail. Turn left on it and soon reach another T junction. Turn right on this looser, wider trail.

Just before reaching the highway, turn left sharply onto a single-track trail heading uphill. Veer left on this single-track trail and reach a dirt road with a stone wall on the other side. Turn right onto the woods road, and soon left onto a narrower trail that heads north. (If you miss this turnoff, you will soon reach a bridge over the highway. This bridge hooks up with more trails, including those in Willowdale State Forest.)

At the next junction, turn left onto a wider trail. Then fork right onto the wider trail. After just about two-tenths of a mile, fork left onto a narrower trail. Take a right fork, rejoin the wider trail, and then turn left just before reaching houses and a field. Ride along this horse farm, following a curving trail, veering right at a fork and, just before a hill, turn right. Keep veering left around this enclosed loop and, just before going downhill, turn right onto a single-track trail. At a T junction turn right, and soon turn right again, reaching the trailhead.

RIDE 23 *DOGTOWN*

This moderate ten-mile loop ride connects jeep roads, grassy double-track trails, and rocky single-track trails in an uninhabited area that was once a colonial English settlement. Now it's a secluded habitat with a varied landscape: a highland woods of small trees, a marshy wetland fed by streams, an other-worldly habitat of ghostly white beech trees, a pine forest, and a reservoir with a narrow old asphalt road circumventing it. There's also a small stone dam, built during the 1930s, which you can ride across while on the Luce Trail.

Large boulders dot the area, including Peter's Pulpit and The Whale's Jaw. But they're overshadowed by the area's claim to fame: several dozen modest-sized boulders with homilies carved into them (on the Babson Boulder Trail). A cen-

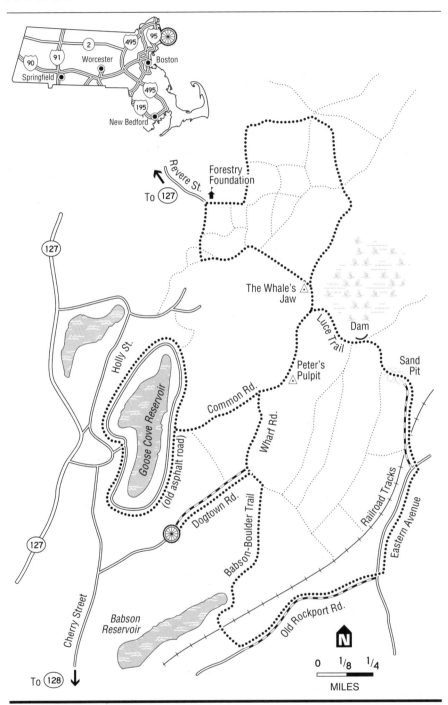

tury after the English colonized this area, which lies a few miles inland from the ocean, they decided that fishing and trading would be easier than farming rock-infested soil. So they moved back to the coast, and the town literally went to the dogs. By the 1930s, Dogtown was inhabited by social outcasts and wild dogs.

Enter local financier and philanthropist, Roger Babson (famous for predicting the stock market crash in 1929). He hired local stonecutters to carve inspirational sayings into the boulders in the area. It's hard to imagine what the down-and-out denizens of Dogtown thought of the rocks crying out, "Get a Job," "Never Try Never Win," "Spiritual Power," "Help Mother," "Ideas," and a dozen other exhortations. As a local naturalist has written: "These carvings give you an idea of what Easter Island would look like if it had been settled by Calvinists." About 40 numerals carved into smaller rocks along dirt roads in Dogtown refer to historic sites that you can look up in the Gloucester Public Library.

Dogtown is located on Cape Ann, a summer vacation spot that also offers the charming towns of Rockport and Gloucester, and several dune-covered public beaches that fill up fast on summer weekends (even though the ocean is chilly). Just south of Gloucester lies Ravenswood Park, a small wooded area with some good trails.

General location: This area is located between the towns of Gloucester and Rockport, 30 miles north of Boston.

Elevation change: The terrain is rolling, with regular short climbs and descents.

Season: Summer and fall are best for riding here; good drainage makes this a spring ride, too.

Services: All services are available in Gloucester, including the Giles of Gloucester bike shop on Maplewood Street, (508) 283-3603.

Hazards: Some of the single-track trails on the eastern side of Dogtown are covered with rocks, making them tricky to "clean."

Rescue index: At most you will be about 1 mile from help.

Land status: Abandoned town roads and public trails.

Maps: A trail map is available for $2 (plus 50 cents postage) from the Gloucester Chamber of Commerce in Gloucester, open weekdays 8 A.M. to 5 P.M. Phone: (617) 283-1601.

Finding the trail: From US 128, cross the Cape Ann Canal, and go around a rotary onto MA 127. Immediately turn right onto Poplar Street and soon left onto Cherry Street. After less than a mile, you will pass a sign on the right for the Cape Ann Sportsmen's Club. A few hundred yards farther, turn right up a patchy asphalt road. Drive slowly on this rugged road, and you will reach a parking area.

Sources of additional information: Local mountain bikers often congregate in the parking area. Also *The Wilds of Cape Ann, A Guide to the Natural Areas of Essex, Gloucester, and Rockport, Massachusetts,* by Eleanor Pope, has information about this historical area.

Notes on the trail: Take the loose-gravel road that climbs out of the parking area (Dogtown Road). When the road veers to the right, fork left onto a single-track trail (Wharf Road), which ends at a double-track trail (Common Road). Turn left on Common Road for a descending side trip to a reservoir. It's a rolling 2-mile ride on an old asphalt road around the reservoir. There's an outlet trail on the north end of the reservoir, or you can double back on Common Road.

Otherwise, turn right on Common Road, pass a large boulder (called Peter's Pulpit) on the right and, after about a half mile, watch for a left fork onto a narrower double-track trail. Fork there and you will reach The Whale's Jaw, a huge boulder in a small clearing (with a marker near it indicating "north"). This is a congregating spot for both hikers and cyclists.

To do a clockwise loop through a pine forest to the north (which is managed by the New England Forestry Foundation), ride around the boulder and pick up a single-track trail. Then turn left at a T junction. Just before a stone wall comes up on the right, turn right onto a single-track trail and enter a pine forest. (If you miss the turnoff you will reach a paved road.) You will come out at the headquarters of the New England Forestry Foundation on Revere Street. To complete a loop through the pine forest, turn right and loop around to the right, returning to The Whale's Jaw from the other direction.

Return to Common Road. For a shorter ride, backtrack to Dogtown Road. Otherwise, turn left on Common Road, then veer right, cross an old dam, and pick up rocky Luce Trail, which passes through a beech forest. You will come out at an active sand pit. You can double back on Luce Trail and attempt 1 of the 3 technical, rock-covered trails that head southwest to the Moraine Trail and Dogtown Road.

Or you can go around the right side of the sand pit, turn right on paved Eastern Avenue, and fork right onto Old Rockport Road, a gated two-wheel-drive dirt road. At the end of this road, turn right into the woods, cross the railroad tracks, and go around the right side of Babson Reservoir. Look for a trail climbing into the woods at the end of the reservoir. You should begin seeing boulders with sayings carved into them, for you're on Babson Boulder Trail. This trail comes out on the Moraine Trail. Turn left and you will reach Dogtown Road on the left.

RIDE 24 *F. GILBERT HILLS STATE FOREST*

This forest, commonly called "Foxboro" state forest, has one of the most extensive networks of single-track trails and woods roads in eastern Massachusetts. This ride is a challenging ten-mile loop marked by green triangular mountain bike signs at intersections. Most of this marked mountain bike ride, created in 1992, uses single-track trails that wind through secluded woods, crisscrossing other trails and gravel roads. (If you don't see a directional sign for a while, just double back and locate the last one you passed.) To do a shorter ride, you can "bail out" on one of several woods roads that intersect the loop (at about five and seven miles).

This forest is undeveloped—it has no two-wheel-drive roads, swimming areas, or camping. Instead, it's an environment of light, sunny woods dotted with granite boulders, a few picnic tables, and a complex network of trails for hiking, biking, and horseback riding. The gravelly terrain covering many of the woods roads is glacial till, left behind when the glaciers melted and withdrew to the north 15,000 years ago. Adjacent Wrentham State Forest is another favorite local mountain biking area.

General location: Just outside Foxboro, 35 miles southwest of Boston.
Elevation change: Although the terrain is relatively flat, there are many regular short climbs and descents.
Season: These well-drained trails (for the most part) and gravel roads provide good riding conditions even in the often wet spring. Summer brings shade, and autumn offers bright foliage.
Services: There is a water spigot at the fire station at forest headquarters. All other services are available in Foxboro.
Hazards: Some of these single-track trails can be difficult; all but expert riders should not hesitate to dismount and walk down steep, eroded stretches. Although one can get disoriented in this "spaghetti" network of trails, the area is compact (about 1,000 acres) and bounded on all sides by paved roads. Also, watch for other trail users.
Rescue index: At most you will be about 1.5 miles from help on secluded trails.
Land status: State forest trails and jeep roads.
Maps: Maps are usually stocked in the main parking lot next to a large trail map on a board. Otherwise, ask for a map from the Department of Environmental Management (see below).
Finding the trail: Take Exit 8 on US 95, and bear right toward Foxboro on Mechanic Street. When you reach the commons in Foxboro, go around it and out the other side onto South Street. After 1.3 miles, turn right onto Mill Street, and then veer left following brown state forest signs. After three-tenths of a mile, you will reach forest parking lots on the right and left. Park in the left-hand lot, which is not gated at dusk.

Sources of additional information:

F. Gilbert Hills State Forest
Mill Street
Foxboro, MA 02035
(508) 543-5850

Department of Environmental Management
Division of Forests and Parks

RIDE 24   F. GILBERT HILLS STATE FOREST

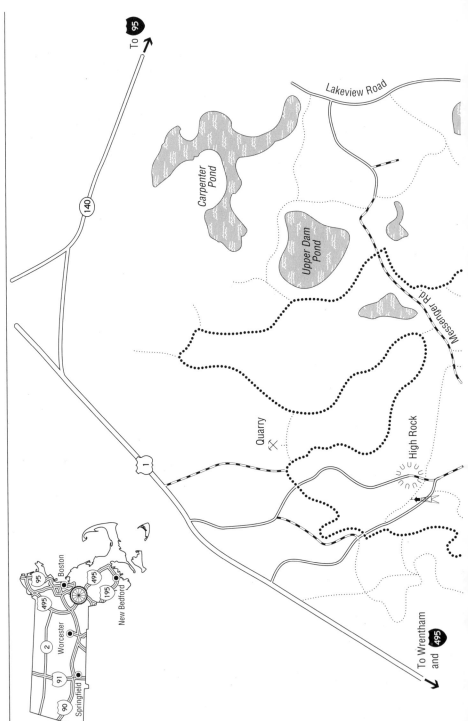

Lakeview Road

To Foxboro

Forest Headquarters

Mill Street

High Rock Road

Messenger Rd.

High Rock Road

Megley Trail

N

MILES

0   1/4   1/2

100 Cambridge Street
Boston, MA 02202
(617) 727-3180

Notes on the trail: This 10-mile loop is marked by green triangular mountain bike signs on trees at intersections. *You must remember to look for these signs— especially at intersections.* Sometimes you will be turning off a wider trail onto a narrower one. If you don't see a green mountain bike sign for a while, turn around and find the last one. The trails on the back side of this loop (the most challenging ones) are also marked by yellow all-terrain-vehicle signs. At several points, you can "bail out" on a gravel road heading back to the parking area.

Head uphill into the woods on a wide path next to the map display board at the main parking lot. Within a few hundred yards, fork right. (This ride comes out on the left-hand fork.) When you reach a T junction, after less than a half mile, turn left, fork left at the next turn, and you will reach paved Granite Street. Directly across the road, pick up the trail, which veers left, crosses the paved road again, and heads onto a dirt woods road, High Rock Road. (You can do a short loop now by making left turns on all dirt roads.)

A few hundred feet along the woods road, turn right onto a single-track trail that heads north. You will reach another dirt road, Messenger Road. Turn right here, and take the first left fork onto another dirt road. Fork left onto the next uphill trail and head north on the left side of Upper Dam Pond, following the trail as it veers south. Just before you reach Messenger Road again, look for a green mountain bike sign on a trail on the right. Keep following the green mountain bike signs. Again, you can shorten this ride by turning southeast on an intersecting dirt road.

RIDE 25 *AMES NOWELL STATE PARK*

This five-mile loop links a hiking trail, several mountain bike trails, and two power line trails in this wooded state park. Riding conditions vary constantly, from fairly easy to somewhat difficult.

You will begin by paralleling a large pond in an environment of mixed hardwoods and softwoods. Then, after cruising on a paved rural road for a half mile, you will explore a power line trail with light vegetation for a short distance, before picking up several single-track trails, and then a double-track trail back to the trailhead (and picnicking area).

Along the way, you cross a wetland and several small streams. Many more trails connect with this loop, including a mostly rideable north-south power line from Braintree to Plymouth.

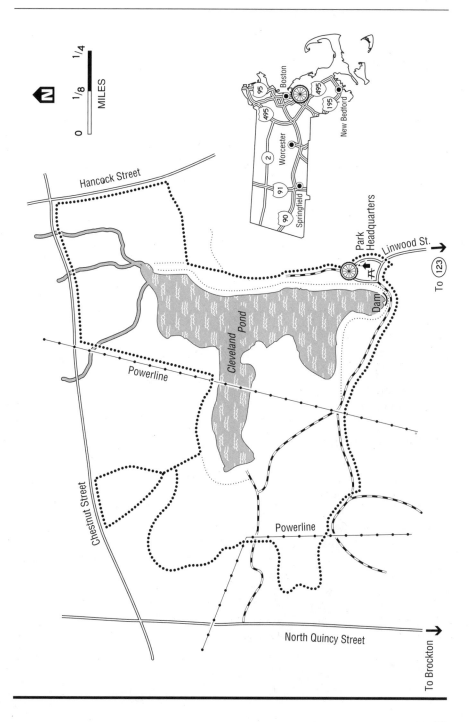

General location: This park is located off MA 24 and MA 3, 20 miles south of Boston.

Elevation change: There are only short climbs and descents on this ride.

Season: Any time between late spring and late fall is good for riding here. You will enjoy the colorful foliage in autumn. Expect some muddy areas in the spring and after a rainfall in any season.

Services: All services are available along MA 18 and in the towns of Abington and Brockton.

Hazards: Watch for occasional obstructions on the more secluded trails.

Rescue index: At most you will be about 1 mile from traveled roads.

Land status: State park trails, a town road, and a power line with a public trail.

Maps: There may be maps available at the entrance, or contact the Department of Environmental Management (see below).

Finding the trail: From MA 3 just south of Boston, take Exit 16B onto MA 18 South, toward Abington. After about 5 miles, turn right onto MA 123 toward Brockton. After eight-tenths of a mile, fork right onto Groveland Street, and then, after 1 mile, turn right onto Linwood Street. You will reach a pair of stone gates at the park entrance. (The main parking lot closes at 4 P.M. Simply park outside the gates if you plan to stay longer.)

Sources of additional information:

Ames Nowell State Park
Linwood Street
Abington, MA (508) 857-5850

Department of Environmental Management
Division of Forests and Parks
100 Cambridge Street
Boston, MA 02202
(617) 727-3180

Notes on the trail: Biking is allowed on all the trails and roads in this park, except for Trail #2, which skirts the eastern shoreline of Cleveland Pond. Although there are plenty of turns on this ride, you can't get too lost, because the area is compact, bounded on all sides by paved roads, and intersected by 2 power lines.

Here's a turn-by-turn description of a 5-mile loop: Pass through the large brown gate on the left side of the parking lot and onto a narrow paved road. (Watch for other park users in this busy area.) Almost immediately, fork right onto an unpaved jeep road.

After about a half mile, just before you reach the pond, turn right onto a single-track trail. You will come out on Hancock Street, a paved rural road. Turn left on it and left at the first major intersection. After about a half mile on this paved road (Chestnut Street), watch for a gated double-track trail on the left at a power line. Turn left onto the power line trail and, after about a half mile, turn right just before the pond.

Single-track solitude. Ames Nowell State Park, Abington, Massachusetts.

After another few tenths of a mile, veer right on the wider trail, and, after another tenth of a mile, turn off this wider trail onto a single-track trail. (You can also follow the wider trail to Chestnut Street. Turn left, and after three-tenths of a mile pick up another trail on the left. Veer right on it, and return to the same spot.)

Follow the single-track trail as it winds around in the woods and comes out on a second power line. Turn left on the power line, and after another two-tenths of a mile turn right off it, and then right almost immediately.

You now will wind around another single-track trail (once a moto-cross trail), and pick up the same power line. Turn right on the power line, and then turn left at a junction with a dirt road. Stay on the dirt road (now heading east), and you will cross the first power line. You can then take the dirt road all the way back to the parking area, or fork left off it onto a single-track trail that runs next to the pond. You will come out at a dam at the pond, cross it, and reach the parking area.

RIDE 26   *WOMPATUCK STATE PARK*

This moderate 8-mile ride circumvents the western half of a large park (3,500 acres) near Boston, with about 10 miles of single- and double-track trails, as well as a winding 12-mile paved bike path. After traveling south on single- and double-track trails, you can loop back on the same trails, or cross over to the eastern side of the park and pick up the paved bike path, cranking all the way back to the trailhead.

This large, accessible park also draws road riders, cross-country skiers, hikers, and campers (400 campsites) to its wooded landscape of oaks and evergreens, old stone walls, a small pond or two, a spring, and several old World War II Navy ammunition bunkers along the paved bike path.

Just east of the park, a trail links up with more trails and unpaved roads in Whitney and Thayer Woods, which is managed by the Trustees of Reservations, a private organization. You might also want to ride to the seacoast towns of Hingham, Cohasset, and Scituate, where you'll find several public beaches and some of the most scenic road riding anywhere. You'll also find another Trustees of Reservations property, World's End, with manicured unpaved roads open for gentle biking.

General location: The park is in Hingham and Cohasset, 20 miles south of Boston.
Elevation change: The ride gains about 150', with an optional climb of another 100'.
Season: Any time between late spring and late fall is good for riding here.
Services: Water is available at Mt. Blue Spring, halfway along the ride on paved Union Street. You will ride past restrooms at the southern side of the large campground, which has 400 sites with showers (open April 15 through October 15). All other services are available along MA 228. A good bike shop is the Bicycle Link on MA 63 in Weymouth, (617) 337-7125.
Hazards: Watch out for occasional obstructions on the trails and the occasional horseback rider. There may be some mosquitoes in low-lying sections in the spring and early summer.
Rescue index: At most you will be about 1 mile from help.
Land status: State park trails and roads.

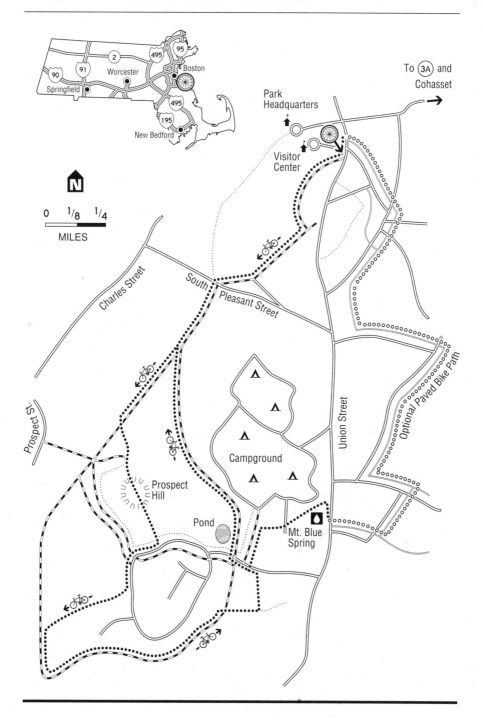

Maps: Maps are available at the Visitor Center (across from the trailhead), or contact the Department of Environmental Management (see below).

Finding the trail: On MA 3 South, take Exit 14 onto MA 28 North toward Cohasset. After about 3 miles, watch for a brown sign for the state park. Turn right just before a handsome white church on the right. After eight-tenths of a mile you will reach a large parking lot on the left and the Visitor Center on the right.

Sources of additional information:

Wompatuck State Park
Union Street
Hingham, MA 02043
(617) 749-7160
Organized mountain bike rides and races are held in this park. Also, you can often hook up with a "show-and-go ride" in the parking lot on weekend mornings.

The Bicycle Link
230 Washington Street (MA 53)
Weymouth, MA 02188
(617) 337-7125

Department of Environmental Management
Division of Forests and Parks
100 Cambridge Street
Boston, MA 02202
(617) 727-3180

Notes on the trail: This ride uses many trails in this area. Although there are a fair number of turns on the ride, it's hard to get lost, since the area is compact and crisscrossed by several paved roads.

Ride up the paved road just past the Visitor Center and turn right into the woods at a sign with trail rules and markings on it. Fork left almost immediately, and then turn sharply right again near the paved road. You will reach a fence on the western border of the park. Veer left on the single-track trail. Soon you will reach a paved road with houses on the right. Turn left onto the road, cross a stream, and immediately turn right onto a jeep road, still heading south.

You can continue doing a loop around the perimeter of the park on this double-track trail. For a more challenging ride, watch for a left turn onto a single-track trail heading uphill. At a T junction at the height-of-land, turn right, and then immediately left.

You will reach a flat, *paved* path at 3 miles. Turn left, pass a concrete bunker on the left and a concrete wall on the right, and reach a paved road. Turn right on it and, after a short distance, watch for a sharp right turn onto another single-track trail. When this trail comes out in a field, veer left in the field and ride back along the tree line and into the woods. Then cross a wooden bridge and reach a T junction at a wider trail (this is the perimeter trail).

Turn left on the double-track trail and, while descending, watch for a single-track trail on the right. Turn right on it and you will reach another T junction, turn left, and reach a paved road. Turn left on the road and almost immediately turn right through an iron gate onto another jeep road (now heading north). You will pass a pond on the left and turn right at a T junction onto an overgrown asphalt road.

When you reach a paved road at the campgrounds, turn right, cross an intersection, pass a restroom building and picnic tables, and turn right through an iron gate onto a jeep road. You will reach a paved road. Turn right and you'll come out in the parking lot at Mt. Blue Spring.

Now you can loop back either by picking up a paved road on the west side of the camping area and bearing left at all intersections, until you reach South Pleasant Street just south of the Visitor Center, or by picking up a paved bike path on the other side of Mt. Blue Street and heading east and north back to the trailhead. For an exploratory ride, try turning south on Union Street and picking up a trail on the left that circumvents a reservoir and eventually heads north.

RIDE 27 *KINGSTON WOODS*

This moderate-to-challenging eight-mile loop ride explores a wooded area on several rugged old roads and a dozen or so single-track trails branching off them. For an easier and simpler ride, you can stay on the woods roads. The single-track trails roll steeply and elaborately on loose rock and sand.

This is a coastal forest, dominated by small pine and oak trees. Climbing a boulder on a short side trail, you can just see the Atlantic Ocean. Another natural feature here is the kettle ponds, small ponds formed about 10,000 years ago when the glaciers melted.

Two miles east of the ride is the seacoast town of Plymouth, where the first English settlers landed at Plymouth Rock. (They weren't the first Europeans to reach the New World, though. Several hundred years before them, Vikings had camped out farther north along the shore. But the Scandinavians decided not to stay. Otherwise, you might be biking in New Sweden.)

In Plymouth, you can tour the Plimouth (original spelling) Plantation, a reconstructed Puritan village, complete with seventeenth-century arts and crafts, and also cruise along the scenic coastline.

General location: This wooded area lies just inland from Plymouth, in the town of Kingston, 40 miles south of Boston.

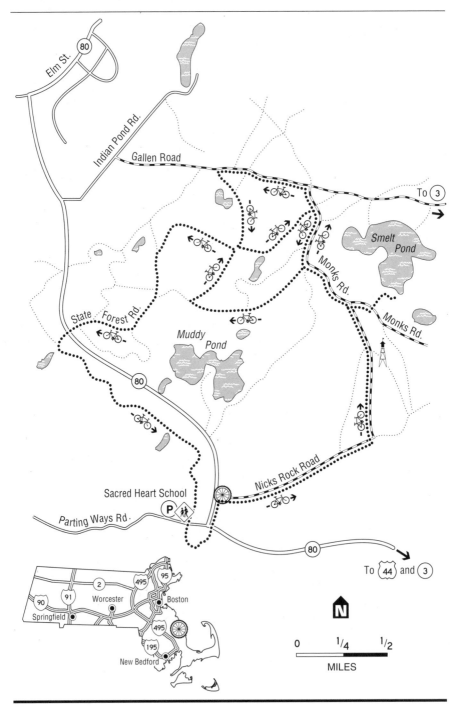

Elm St.

80

Indian Pond Rd.

Gallen Road

To 3

Smelt Pond

Monks Rd.

State Forest Rd.

Monks Rd.

Muddy Pond

80

Nicks Rock Road

Sacred Heart School

P

Parting Ways Rd.

80

To 44 and 3

2

495

95

Worcester

Boston

90

91

Springfield

495

195

New Bedford

N

0   1/4   1/2

MILES

Elevation change: The terrain is flat, with a few small hills.

Season: Riding here is best between May and late fall. Local cyclists also ride during the winter, if the snow is not too deep. In the spring and after a rainfall you will encounter a few large mudholes.

Services: All services are available along MA 44 and in Kingston and Plymouth. At the junction of MA 3 and MA 44, signs indicate which directions to go for tourist information, camping, and historic areas. Carver Cycles bike shop is located at the junction of MA 44 and MA 58 in Carver, (508) 866-4033.

Hazards: Watch for some loose sand and the occasional motorized off-road vehicle.

Rescue index: At most you will be about 2 miles from help.

Land status: The paths in these woods are old town roads and trails on private land owned by the Sisters of Divine Providence (located across from the trailhead), with public access permitted.

Maps: The best map of this area is in a book of maps, *Atlas of Metropolitan Boston and Eastern Massachusetts,* Universal Publishing Company. However, some of these trails are documented only in this mountain biking book.

Finding the trail: Take Exit 6 off MA 3 and turn left onto MA 44. After 1.4 miles, turn right onto MA 80 East. After another 1.4 miles, MA 80 East turns sharply right at a large high school. You can park in the high school lot. About two-tenths of a mile farther on MA 80 there is a large building on the left and a narrow dirt road heading into the woods on the right. This is the trailhead.

Sources of additional information:

New England Mountain Bike Association (NEMBA)
69 Spring Street
Cambridge, MA 02141
(617) 497-6891

Notes on the trail: You might want to explore this area in 2 stages. First, familiarize yourself with the layout of the woods roads and double-track trails. Then return to explore some of the more convoluted single-track trails. The area is compact and bordered on the west by MA 80.

Take the woods road from MA 80 until you reach a T junction after a little more than a mile. Turn right to reach a large sand mining area that is rideable. You can climb a large boulder there for a modest view of the Atlantic Ocean. Go back to the T junction, turn left onto another woods road, fork right at an island, and you will reach another T junction at Monks Road. (For a short side trip to a public beach at a pond, turn right, then left at a graded dirt road at a clearing, and left again.)

Turn left on Monks Road and keep bearing right, passing Smelt Pond on the right, until you reach another T junction. Turn left sharply onto Gallen Road. (If you turn right on Gallen Road you will reach Independence Mall on MA 3 after a mile, where you can eat, shop, or see a movie. Bring along a bike lock.)

Now you can weave around on narrower trails. Here's one configuration: While descending on Gallen Road, after less than a mile, turn left sharply onto a double-track trail. (If you go straight you will reach a paved road at MA 80). You pass a small pond on the right and reach a 4-way intersection. Turn left sharply uphill, reach a T junction just before rejoining Gallen Road, turn right, and backtrack for a short distance on Monks Road. Then turn right up a single-track trail, stay to the left when you reach a pond, and you will come out a T junction with State Forest Road. You can continue in the same direction on this unpaved road to MA 80 and turn left.

Or, turn right and bear right almost immediately. Just before a woods road intersection, turn left onto a single-track, which passes a pond, until you come out on a double-track trail. Turn left and rejoin State Forest Road. Turn right on this woods road and reach MA 80 after 1 mile.

You can take MA 80 back to the trailhead. To do another mile or two of single-track, though, cross MA 80 and take a dirt road to the right. Almost immediately, turn left onto a single-track trail. Stay on the trail in the woods, forking left at a tree with orange dots on it. You will cross paved Parting Ways Road. Take the trail across the road, turn left onto a double-track trail, and come out at the high school at the junction of Parting Ways Road and MA 80.

RIDE 28 *CRANBERRY RUN*

This fairly challenging 18.5-mile ride begins at an old mill site, cruises through inhabited countryside, and picks up a flat rail-trail. After a few miles, the ride switches to a power line trail through light vegetation, with some views of cranberry bogs. Then it reenters the woods, passes a horse farm, and comes out in the suburbs. The second half of the ride runs mainly through light woods.

In other words, there's a bit of everything on this ride: several miles on a smooth rail-trail, a mile or two on sandy single-track, about nine miles on single-track trails in the woods, and short stretches on paved roads. You can shorten the ride by eliminating several side loops on single-track trails.

This region (southeastern Massachusetts) produces most of the world's cranberries. These tart fruits grow in low-lying, flooded bogs bordered by small moats. An entirely natural phenomenon also occurs each spring, when spawning alewife fish head upstream by the thousands, passing the mill site at the trailhead, where people gather to catch them—by the bucketful.

General location: This ride begins in Middleboro and crosses into Plymouth; it is 40 miles south of Boston.

Elevation change: The terrain is relatively flat, with a dozen or so short steep climbs and descents.

Season: This is a good 4-season ride—if you don't mind a bit of mud (in the spring) or snow and ice.

Services: At the easternmost end of the ride there's a convenience grocery store on MA 58. Food and other services are also available at the rotary on MA 144. There's a private campground across from the trailhead, and a nearby bike shop, Carver Cycles, is located at the junction of MA 44 and MA 58 in Carver, (508) 866-4033.

Hazards: Be prepared for riding conditions to change from a smooth, flat path to tight single-track, then to soft sand in places, and to intersections with paved roads.

Rescue index: At most you will be about a half mile from homes and traveled roads.

Land status: A railroad right-of-way, a power line, and private land with public access allowed on the trails.

Maps: This book contains the only published map of this ride. A detailed state road map (or collection of such maps) will show the crossroads.

Finding the trail: Take Exit 6 on Interstate 495 South, onto US 44 East toward Middleboro and Plymouth. Go around the rotary and continue on US 44. ("Rotaries" are unsignalled, circular, first-come, first-serve intersections. Vehicles already in the rotary or on the right have the legal right-of-way. They're not just intersections—they're adventures.) Watch for a large old mill site on the right at a light. Turn right and park next to the mill site.

Sources of additional information:

New England Mountain Bike Association (NEMBA)
69 Spring Street
Cambridge, MA 02141
(617) 497-6891

Notes on the trail: This ride has many turns. Be prepared to stop, scan your surroundings, and read these directions and the map. Begin on paved Plymouth Street, just across from the mill parking lot. Ride for 1 mile east on this scenic, farm-dotted road, until you reach a large man-made pond on the right. Turn left there onto a gravel road.

At the end of the road, turn right onto a narrower road between pine trees. This is the beginning of the rail-trail. (Beginners can do an easy out-and-back ride along this flat trail.) A few hundred feet farther, turn left toward the highway, and immediately right onto a single-track trail (which might be marked with orange blazes). This trail parallels the rail-trail. After about 1.5 miles on it, you will rejoin the rail-trail on the right.

Next, you cross a paved road, with a 275-year-old cemetery on the other side. When the trail reaches US 44 on the left, veer to the right up a short, steep hill,

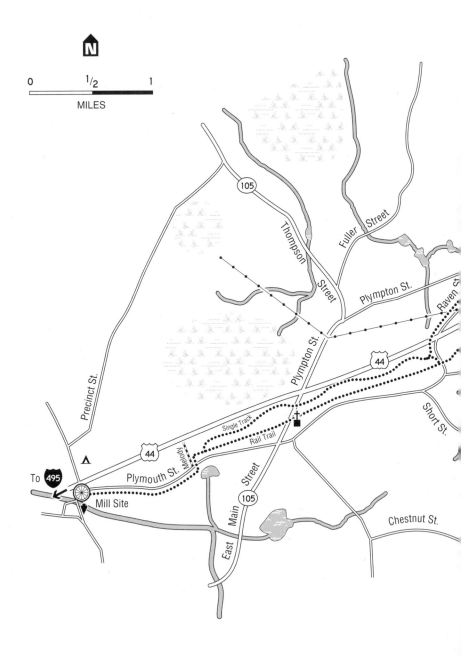

A warm-up stretch on a rail-trail. Middleboro, Massachusetts.

onto the power line trail. When the power line trail reaches a paved road, you can continue straight on the trail, but you will encounter a swampy area with a swampy trail around it. Instead, turn right onto the paved road, then left at the first stop sign. You'll pass a cranberry bog on the right. At the other end of the bog, turn left onto a jeep road, and immediately right up a single-track trail that rejoins the power line trail.

About 5 miles into the ride, a few hundred feet before another paved road, watch for a left turn onto a single-track trail. Turn left, bear left at the tree line, and you're doubling back on a trail that parallels the power line. After about a mile, veer right into the woods on a winding single-track trail, and right again at a T junction. Veer right again onto a small power line trail and follow it past some horse stables. After crossing pavement, bear left on the main trail.

After a few hundred yards, turn right off this trail onto a double-track trail. Then turn right at a fork, veer right down a dirt road, pass a house, and come out on a paved road (Fuller Street). Turn left on it. (To take a side trip on dirt roads around a cranberry bog, turn right at a sign at the end of the cranberry bog on the right.) At the next paved T junction, turn left and you'll soon reach a convenience store on the right on MA 58. Congratulations, for you've made it halfway.

Continue on MA 58 (Main Street) to the left (north), through a major intersection with a stoplight, and immediately turn left into the parking lot of a shopping center. Stay to the right in the rear of the parking lot and pick up the rail-trail on the right. After a short distance, you will be riding on a paved road that covers the rail-trail; continue on it past a sand pit, until it ends near US 44. Cross US 44 and turn right into the woods on the other side of the highway (where the guardrail ends) onto a single-track trail. (It is illegal to ride on US 44.)

Follow this winding trail, passing more cranberry bogs on the right. Bear left at a ditch near the highway and continue on the trail, paralleling the highway. Continue heading west, past a large cranberry bog on the right. Now watch for single-track trails veering off to the left and right. You can continue straight on the rail-trail or take one or both single-track loops (which are dirt-bike trails). Both loops return to the rail-trail.

You will reach a fence and a steep downhill at Carmel Street. Cross the paved road and pick up the trail again. Bear left on a double-track trail. (Another optional side loop comes up on the left.) Ride around a cranberry bog on the left, through a clearing, past some homes, and onto a paved road. Turn left and immediately left again onto unpaved Raven Street. A few hundred yards farther, be sure to take the left fork, which is Raven Street (the right fork is a driveway). Cross a power line and continue on this jeep road, reaching US 44. Cross the highway again and turn right on a single-track trail. Again, after a few hundred feet, you can take either the rail-trail or the single-track to return to the trailhead.

RIDE 29 *MYLES STANDISH STATE FOREST*

This 16,000-acre forest is one of the largest pine barrens in the country. Pine barrens are aquifers; the purest known water is stored beneath these vast expanses of pines and oaks. (There's a spigot at the trailhead.) This challenging seven-mile loop ride explores this unusual "minimalist" habitat, which is dotted with 35 small ponds called kettle ponds, formed some 10,000 years ago when the glaciers retreated north. In spring and fall the forest is also a stopover for migrating birds.

RIDE 29 *MYLES STANDISH STATE FOREST*

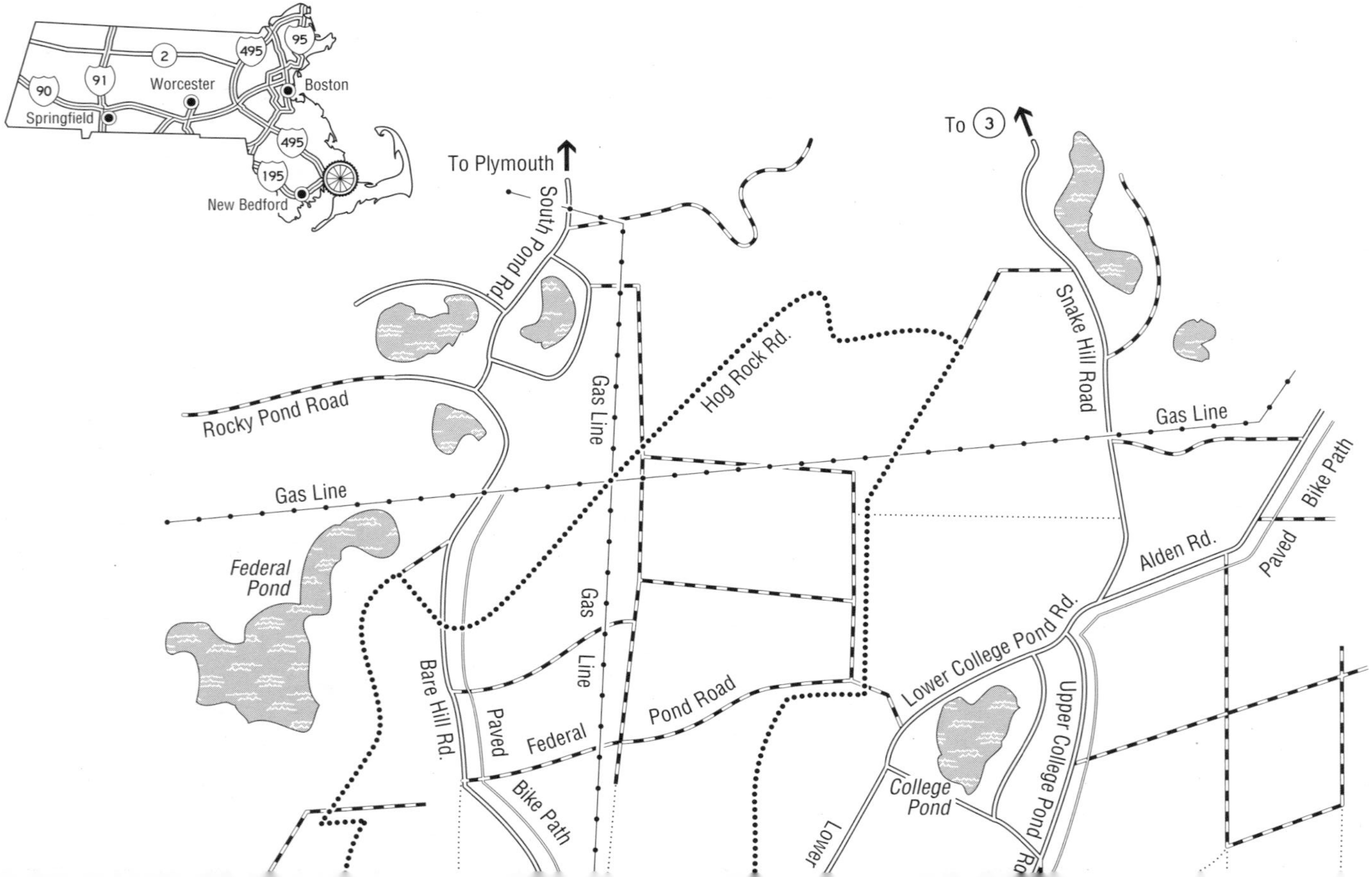

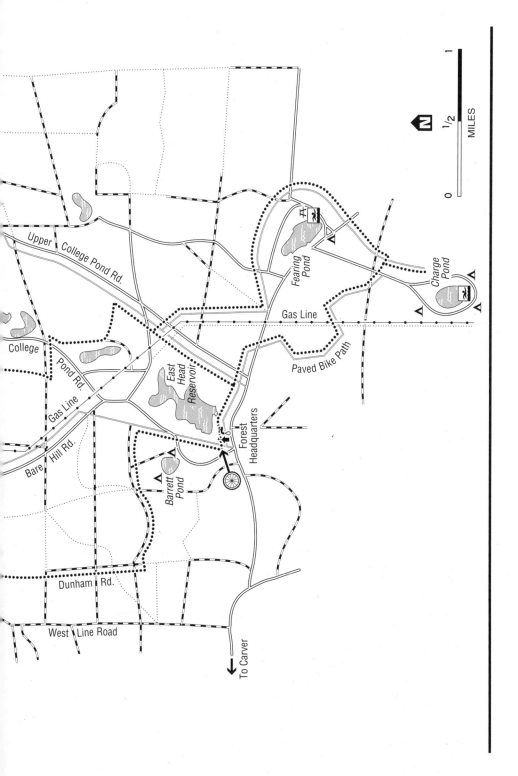

Upper College Pond Rd.

College

Pond Rd.

Gas Line

Bare Hill Rd.

East
Head
Reservoir

Fearing
Pond

Charge
Pond

Gas Line

Paved Bike Path

Forest
Headquarters

Barrett
Pond

Dunham Rd.

West Line Road

To Carver

N

MILES

0   ½   1

The 30 or so miles of trails and unpaved roads in this forest vary from hard-packed dirt to grass and loose sand. Some of the sandier terrain can be difficult riding. In general, trails designated with red markers (bridal paths for horseback riding) are less sandy than some of the unpaved roads. There's also a rolling 15-mile paved bike path that follows the contours of the land.

Two of the ponds in the forest have swimming beaches, and just outside the forest you can cruise by cranberry bogs on paved roads. This region produces more cranberries than any other place in the world. You might also want to visit Plymouth, four miles to the east. There you can tour Plimouth (original spelling) Plantation, a reconstructed Puritan village. The forest also lies only 15 miles from the beginning of Cape Cod (at the Cape Cod Canal in Bourne). Myles Standish, who was not a Pilgrim, arrived on the *Mayflower*, and became the military leader of the Plymouth Colony.

General location: The forest straddles the towns of Plymouth and Carver, 45 miles south of Boston.

Elevation change: The terrain is relatively flat, but there are many short climbs and descents.

Season: You can ride in this area year-round. The sandy trails are well drained in the spring, and there is usually little snow in the winter. Although summer can be hot, you can cool off at swimming ponds.

Services: Water is available at the trailhead (outside the forest headquarters). A nearby bike shop is Carver Cycles, at the junction of MA 44 and MA 58 in Carver, (508) 866-4033. The forest has several hundred campsites, available from mid-April to mid-October, with showers ($12 per night, no reservations). There is also a grocery store with a deli a few miles from the trailhead, toward South Carver.

Hazards: Although the trails and roads in this area are distinct, they are also plentiful and often resemble each other; carrying a map and compass is a good idea. Also, bring plenty of water, especially during the summer. (There is a spigot at the forest headquarters.)

Rescue index: At most you will be several miles from help on secluded trails.

Land status: State forest trails and roads. *Note:* Biking is not allowed along the shorelines of the ponds, nor in one area marked for hikers only, nor on the groomed cross-country ski trails during the winter.

Maps: Maps are available at the forest headquarters or from the Department of Environmental Management (see below).

Finding the trail: From the north, take Exit 5 off MA 3. Turn right onto Long Pond Road and follow the brown state forest signs for about 3 miles, until you reach the paved access road on the right. This road runs diagonally through the forest for 5 miles. (It's a good way to familarize yourself with the area and several intersecting trailheads.) Note the paved bike path on the left, which parallels the road. From the west and south, take Exit 2 (South Carver) on Interstate 495. Follow MA 58 into South Carver, and then brown signs into the forest.

Miles of secluded roads through a pine barren. Myles Standish State Forest, Plymouth, Massachusetts.

Sources of additional information:

Myles Standish State Forest
Cranberry Road
South Carver, MA 02633
(508) 866-2526

Department of Environmental Management
Division of Forest and Parks
100 Cambridge Street
Boston, MA 02202
(617) 727-3180

Notes on the trail: There are dozens of options for riding here. This is one large loop through several areas. From the parking lot at forest headquarters (where you can pick up a trail map), take the paved bike path heading northwest, behind and to the left of the headquarters. You will cross a paved road, and then turn left off the paved bike path at the first intersection with an unpaved, sandy jeep road (Barrett Road). At a stop sign, turn left and almost immediately right into a parking area. Follow the ATV (all-terrain-vehicle) signs at the other side of the parking lot onto a narrow double-track trail.

At a 4-way intersection, get off this trail (which becomes eroded) and onto the dirt road heading in the same direction on the right. After about another half mile, you will reach an intersection with another wide jeep road, Dunham Road. Turn right on it, and ride for about a mile and a half on this sandy, rolling road, crossing a couple of other unpaved roads (which you can take to the right for a shorter ride), until you reach T junction with Federal Pond Road.

You can do a longer, more challenging loop by turning left onto Federal Pond Road, and then right at the next junction, onto West Line Road. Follow the yellow dirt-bike signs past Federal Pond on the left and, as you pass the pond, veer off the main road onto a narrower trail on the right. You will cross a paved road, the paved bike path (which you can take back to the trailhead), and a gas line. Now you're on a secluded trail on the northern edge of the forest, which winds southward, eventually reaching Federal Pond Road.

You now have 3 options for returning to the trailhead: jeep roads, narrower bridal paths, and the paved bike path. One way back is to turn right onto Federal Pond Road and pick up a bridal path on the left. This trail will reach a T junction with unpaved Three Cornered Pond Road. Turn left on it, and soon reach paved Lower College Pond Road. Turn right on the pavement for a short distance, and pick up a trail on the other side going uphill to the right.

At the top of the hill, with a pond on the right, turn left onto a bridal path (red markers) named Negas Road. This trail will intersect the paved bike path just before reaching Upper College Pond Road. Turn right on the bike path and follow signs painted on it for headquarters, or head southeast on the bike path toward Fearing Pond and Charge Pond.

The *15-mile paved bike path* has 3 main sections: one heading northwest for 4 miles, one northeast for 5 miles, and several interconnecting loops to the south for 6 miles. The 4-mile out-and-back path heading northwest is more rolling and faster than the longer out-and-back ride to the northeast.

To do a 5-mile loop to the south, ride due east on the paved access road from forest headquarters. The bike path comes up on the left at a brown gate. After less than a half mile turn right at a fork in the path and then right again at the next fork.

After crossing 2 paved roads and a parking area, you will reach a T junction. Turn right to do a side trip to Charge Pond. Or turn left to continue on the loop. After another mile and a half or so, you will reach another swimming pond,

Fearing Pond. After passing the pond, white signs painted on the path at an intersection indicate several destinations: forest headquarters, Charge Pond, and Plymouth.

RIDE 30 *FREETOWN / FALL RIVER STATE FOREST*

This 6,500-acre forest is a favorite mountain biking area in southeastern Massachusetts. It has several dozen miles of trails and unpaved roads, including a challenging 23-mile single-track loop marked with yellow signs. The moderate 15-mile loop ride that I suggest connects a variety of paths: double-track trails, single-track trails, two-wheel-drive dirt and gravel roads, and a gas line trail. At several junctions, you can take side trips that create longer, more difficult rides, or shorter easier ones. Exploring this forest will give you a taste of a coastal habitat, with its hard-packed, sandy ground and landscape dominated by small pine and oak trees.

About halfway on the ride (at the junction of Copicut Road and Bell Rock Road), you will pass a sign explaining that this area is part of the Wampanoag Indian Reservation. Like most Native American tribes in the Northeast, the Wampanoags now hold powwows—public chanting, dancing, and crafts events—at various times during the year.

General location: The forest straddles the towns of Freetown and Fall River.
Elevation change: This terrain is flat, except for regular short, steep hills on the single-track.
Season: This is a 4-season ride, if there has been little snow and not too much wetness in the spring.
Services: Restrooms and a drinking fountain are available near the parking lot. All other services are in Freetown and Fall River.
Hazards: Be ready to change riding techniques when switching from smooth dirt roads to rugged, narrow trails.
Rescue index: At most you will be about 1 mile from help on secluded trails.
Land status: Old town roads and state forest trails.
Maps: There is a large trail map on a board at the parking lot, or you can have a map mailed to you from the Department of Environmental Management (see below).
Finding the trail: Take Exit 10 off MA 24 and turn right toward signs for Profile Rock and Freetown State Forest. After a half mile, turn left in Assonet at a sign for the state forest. Almost immediately, fork right at another sign for the forest. At 1.5 miles, you will pass Profile Rock on the left. At 2.5 miles, turn right at a

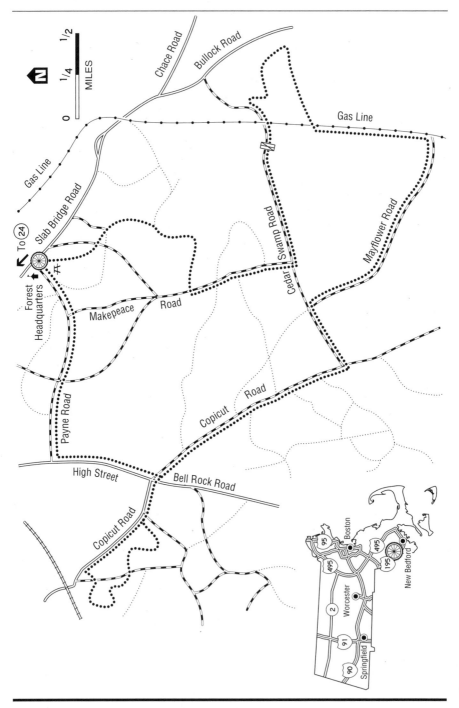

Log-hopping—with room to spare. Freetown/Fall River State Forest, Fall River, Massachusetts.

brown sign for the forest, drive up the paved access road, and turn left into a large paved parking lot across from the forest headquarters.

Sources of additional information:

Freetown State Forest
P.O. Box 171
Assonet, MA 02702
(508) 644-5522

Department of Environmental Management
Division of Forests and Parks
100 Cambridge Street
Boston, MA 02202
(617) 727-3180

Notes on the trail: This fairly long ride has many turns on it because it explores many areas in this forest. For an easier ride, stay on the dirt roads. For more difficult riding, take the marked single-track trails, mainly west of Copicut Road.

Ride past several picnic tables and pick up a double-track trail heading southeast. Turn right at a T junction, fork left, and go straight through a 4-way intersection. (For a more challenging ride, turn right at the 4-way intersection and soon fork left onto a single-track trail, which rejoins this loop farther along it.)

At the next T junction with a wide two-wheel-drive dirt road, Makepeace Road, turn left. Turn left again onto another two-wheel-drive road, Cedar Swamp Road. You will pass through a large brown gate. Cross the gas line (locals claim it's rideable), and you will come out at a large clearing.

Bear right along the tree line and head into the woods on a trail. Then bear left on an old road, and watch for a sharp right onto another trail, and then fork right again. You will join up with the gas line trail heading in the same direction. Take the next hard right turn off the gas line, onto a distinct woods road, Mayflower Road. (In midsummer this path is lined with mayflowers, the state flower. Although it's not endangered, it's not common any longer.)

You will pass through another brown forest gate and reach Cedar Swamp Road. (You can take the fairly easy single-track trail on the other side, which rejoins the loop on Copicut Road.) Otherwise, turn left on the road and right at the next woods road, Copicut Road. You will reach a paved 4-way intersection. (For a shorter ride, turn right onto High Street. For a longer ride, turn left onto Bell Rock Road.)

Head straight on Copicut Road, take the second left onto a single-track trail, and immediately veer right on it. Twist and turn along this single-track trail, cross a wide dirt road, and continue on the trail. Take the next right turn, go through an intersection, turn left at a T junction, and you will reach Copicut Road. Turn right, and right again on paved High Street. Ride downhill and turn right at a forest sign onto unpaved Payne Road.

For a longer, more difficult ride, turn left at the second metal gate on Payne Road, turn right several times, and rejoin either Payne Road or Makepeace Road. Otherwise, ride straight on Payne Road, fork left at an intersection, and reach the parking lot.

RIDE 31   *MASHPEE RIVER WOODLANDS*

Want to do some easy, yet stimulating, single-track riding on Cape Cod? These five or so miles of narrow, rolling trails will fit the bill. Beginner riders will be moderately challenged by these winding, up-and-down paths, while experienced mountain bikers will appreciate the tight turns and occasional log jumps. For a longer ride, try doing the trails in both directions. Because this is conservation land along a scenic river, expect to meet an occasional hiker or two on the trails. The Mashpee are a Native American tribe that still lives on Cape Cod.

Another easy off-road ride on the Cape circumvents Nickerson State Park in Brewster (to the east), using about seven miles of dirt roads and double-track trails. This state park is also a popular camping site. (For more information, call (508) 896-3491.)

For more challenging riding on the Cape, there's the Trail of Tears in Sandwich, as well as other informal sites, which you can learn about by dropping in at a local bike shop. Or, for a change, pump up the tires and check out the paved 20-mile-long Cape Cod Rail Trail, which runs from Dennis to Eastham.

General location: This conservation land is located in the town of Mashpee.

Elevation change: Although this is flat terrain, the main trail rolls up and down.

Season: You can ride here any time between late spring and late fall.

Services: All services are available in Mashpee and along MA 28. Two nearby mountain bike shops are: True Wheel Cycles in Pocasset, (508) 564-4807, and Corner Cycle in Falmouth, (508) 540-4195.

Hazards: Less experienced riders should slow down around the steep curves on these tight, winding trails to avoid close encounters with trees. Also, watch out for hikers on blind turns. This is a conservation area, so be sure not to leave tire tracks.

Rescue index: You will be near well-traveled roads.

Land status: Trails in a public park.

Maps: There is a large trail map and a map box on a board at the trailhead.

Finding the trail: Travel US 6 across the Sagamore Bridge onto Cape Cod, and after 4 miles take Exit 2 onto MA 130 South, toward Mashpee and Sandwich. After about 8.5 miles, turn right onto MA 28. Continue for just under 2 miles, then turn left sharply onto Quinaquisset Avenue. (This road is three-tenths of a mile east of the rotary [the traffic circle] in Mashpee.) You will pass a sign on the right for the Mashpee River Woodlands/North Parking Lot. You can park there, or you can continue until you reach Mashpee Neck Road, turn right, and watch for a parking area on the right at another sign: "Mashpee River Woodlands."

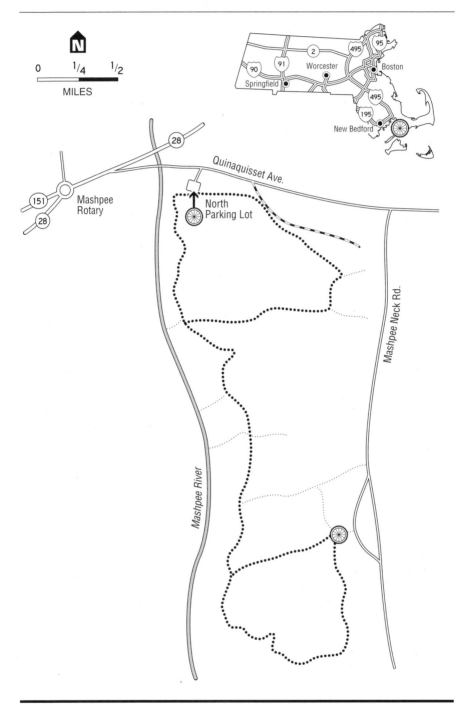

Winding, rolling single-track. Mashpee River Woodlands, Mashpee, Massachusetts.

Sources of additional information:

Corner Cycle
115 Palmer Avenue
Falmouth, MA 02540
(508) 540-4195

Notes on the trail: You can't get lost for long in this compact area: to the east lies paved Mashpee Neck Road, and to the west runs the Mashpee River. There's 1 main trail paralleling the river to the north, while 2 loops, the Chickadee Trail and the Partridge Berry Trail, make up the southern part of the ride.

RIDE 32   *LAGOON POND—LAKE TASHMOO*

This ten-mile ride explores a half-dozen dirt roads and as many trails in one section of Martha's Vineyard, a large island just off Cape Cod. The ride begins and ends at the ferry landing in the town of Vineyard Haven, so you can get off the boat and ride.

Within a mile or so, you're on a dirt road running along a lagoon (a salty body of water separated from the ocean by a sandbar). After rolling along double-track trails in an inland forest and a handsome old unpaved road, you end up at a public beach on Vineyard Sound. Finally, you can return to the town of Vineyard Haven, for either a snack or a gourmet meal, or ride on a power line trail to another coastal view, The Loop at the tip of West Chop.

For mountain bikers, Martha's Vineyard beckons in any season. (It's less crowded and less expensive in the off-season, between Labor Day and Memorial Day). It's worth staying a couple of days, too, to explore more areas, like Gay Head, Oak Bluffs, and Chilmark, where there's also off-road riding. *Note:* During the summer, riding the wrong way on a one-way street in Vineyard Haven is illegal—and it is enforced.

General location: This ride loops through Tisbury and Vineyard Haven.
Elevation change: The terrain is relatively flat, with only short, gradual climbs and descents.
Season: You can do this loop in any season. Between Memorial Day and Labor Day, the Vineyard is much more crowded with cars and mopeds. The off-season weather can be milder than the mainland.
Services: All services are available in Vineyard Haven. Two bike shops are present: Cycle Works in Vineyard Haven, (508) 693-6966, and Edgartown Bicycle in Edgartown, (508) 627-9008. Two private campgrounds can be reached at (508) 693-3772 and (508) 693-0233. A good bed-and-breakfast is High Haven House: (800) 232-9204 or (508) 693-9204 in Massachusetts.
Hazards: Watch for traffic at crossroads, especially during the summer. You might want to bring some insect repellent in the early summer.
Rescue index: You are never far from houses and traveled roads.
Land status: Active town roads and public trails.
Maps: An excellent map of all the roads and many of the trails on the Vineyard is called simply "Martha's Vineyard." This green-and-brown map, published by Vineyard native J. Donovan, is available in many stores on the island.
Finding the trail: The ride begins at the ferry landing in Vineyard Haven. To reach Martha's Vineyard, you take a ferry from Woods Hole on the southwestern tip of Cape Cod. The fare is $4.50 one-way (May 15–October 14) or $4.00

RIDE 32 *LAGOON POND-LAKE TASHMOO*

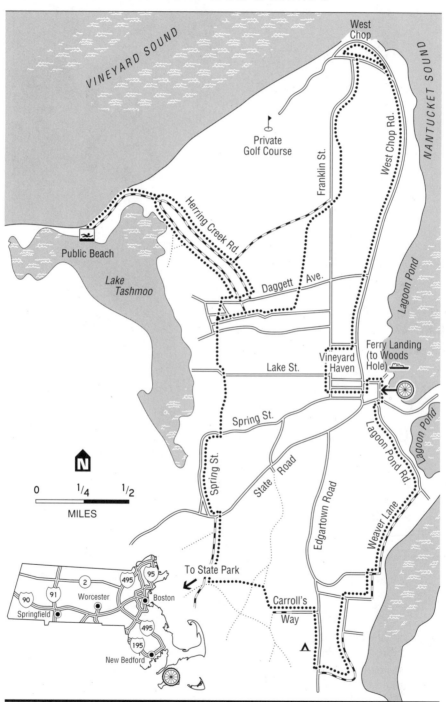

Riding on a divided "highway." Martha's Vineyard, Massachusetts.

in the off-season. Bikes are $2.75 one-way. Ferries leave hourly from 7:15 A.M. to 10 P.M.

Note: The ferry parking lot at Woods Hole is often full. Instead, you must park at a lot 4 miles away in Falmouth, at $6 per day, and take a free shuttle bus to and from the ferry. Or you can do as some cyclists (and cycling authors) do: find a safe and legal parking spot just outside Woods Hole and bike to the ferry. For more ferry information call (508) 540-2022. The Bonanza Bus Line, (800) 556-3815, runs from Boston, Providence, RI, and New York City, to Woods Hole. Space permitting, it takes bikes for $2.50.

Sources of additional information:

Vineyard Offroad Bicycling Assocation (VORBA)
(508) 693-4905 or (508) 693-1878
This club holds group rides for all ability levels.

Martha's Vineyard Chamber of Commerce
P.O. Box 1698, Beach Road
Vineyard Haven, MA 02568
(508) 693-0085

Notes on the trail: This ride links many roads and trails; a map of the Vineyard will help you stay oriented. You begin by turning left at the ferry landing and riding south on Water Street, which becomes Lagoon Pond Road. You will pass a "Dead End" sign. Just before you come to a fork, turn right onto gated Weaver Lane. (It says "private road" but it's not; they just don't want a lot of traffic.)

This road becomes two-wheel-drive. Fork left on it, veer right, climb, and turn left at the first intersection. This road becomes paved. Turn left again onto another dirt road, keep going straight onto a narrower dirt road, and you will come out on paved Edgartown Road.

Turn right and ride on the bike path along the other side of the road. Pass a private campground and turn left onto paved Carroll's Way. This road becomes unpaved. Fork left onto a double-track trail where the road ends. At a T junction, turn right on a graded jeep trail, and left at the next junction. You will come to a 4-way junction with another jeep trail.

You can continue on the trail you're riding to the southwest, and come out on Old County Road just above the state park (see the Martha's Vineyard State Park ride, Ride 33). Otherwise, turn right on the wider trail. You will come out on a paved road; turn left, and after a few hundred feet turn right onto paved Spring Street.

After making a sharp right-hand turn, watch for a power line trail on the left. Turn left onto this trail. You will cross a paved road, and then come out on another paved road that veers to the right. Go straight, staying on the power line for a few yards, and then fork left onto a narrower trail. This trail comes out after a few hundred feet on a paved cul-de-sac. Turn right, then left at the next paved T junction.

At the end of this cul-de-sac, pick up a trail on the right, and after a few hundred feet turn left onto an old dirt road, Herring Creek Road. Follow this road until it ends at a public beach on Lake Tashmoo.

Turn around and ride back up the dirt road. Now you can retrace the ride back to the power line, turn left, and ride on this sandy trail. Cross 2 paved roads, until the trail comes out on Franklin Street near West Chop. (Avoid the last stretch of the power line, which comes out on private property.) Take the paved loop around this scenic point (obeying the traffic signals on this one-way street). And then return to Vineyard Haven on West Chop Road. Otherwise, take any one of several paved roads from the end of the dirt road you took to the beach at Lake Tashmoo, and return to Vineyard Haven.

RIDE 33 *MARTHA'S VINEYARD STATE PARK*

This 15-mile loop ride explores a sunny, quiet forest in the heart of Martha's Vineyard. Its 4,000-plus acres of pines, oaks, blueberry bushes, and low-lying ground cover are crisscrossed by about 30 miles of fire roads and more challenging double-track and single-track trails. It's a good place for novice riders, since it's flat and usually smooth. But accomplished riders will find it fun—and fast.

The ride alternates between unpaved fire lanes, single-track and double-track trails, and a few stretches on paved bike paths. Almost all of the paths are hard-packed sand. No motorized vehicles are allowed in the park, so it's a tranquil environment where you might see many kinds of birds and meet up with hikers (from a nearby youth hostel) and horseback riders. In summer, it's the calm eye of the hurricane of bustling activity on this popular island.

General location: The ride is located in the middle of Martha's Vineyard, about 2.5 miles south of the ferry landing in the town of Vineyard Haven.
Elevation change: The terrain here is flat, with only occasional short dips and hills.
Season: This ride can be done in all 4 seasons. You might carry an insect repellent in the early summer and late fall. Also, between Memorial Day and Labor Day the roads on the island (as well as Cape Cod) are busy. The off-season is a good time to visit Martha's Vineyard, since it's less expensive and the weather is milder than on the mainland.
Services: All services are available in Vineyard Haven, Oak Bluffs, and other towns. There are two bike shops nearby: Cycle Works in Vineyard Haven, (508) 693-6966, and Edgartown Bicycle in Edgartown, (508) 627-9008. There is no camping in the state park, but 2 private campgrounds can be reached at (508) 693-3772 and (508) 693-0233. A good bed-and-breakfast is High Haven House, (800) 232-9204 or (508) 693-9204 in Massachusetts.
Hazards: None, but watch for occasional horseback riders and hikers. Also, in early spring and late fall, ticks can be living in the woods, so it's best not to wander around in the underbrush. There's also some poison ivy growing among the blueberry bushes.
Rescue index: At most, you will be about 2 miles from help on easily traversed but secluded roads and trails.
Land status: Trails and fire lanes in a state park. (The formal name for this park is the Manuel F. Correlius State Park. However, it is commonly known, even on maps, as Martha's Vineyard State Park.)
Maps: An excellent map of all the roads and many of the trails on the Vineyard is called simply "Martha's Vineyard." This green-and-brown folding map, published by Vineyard native J. Donovan, is available in many stores on the island.

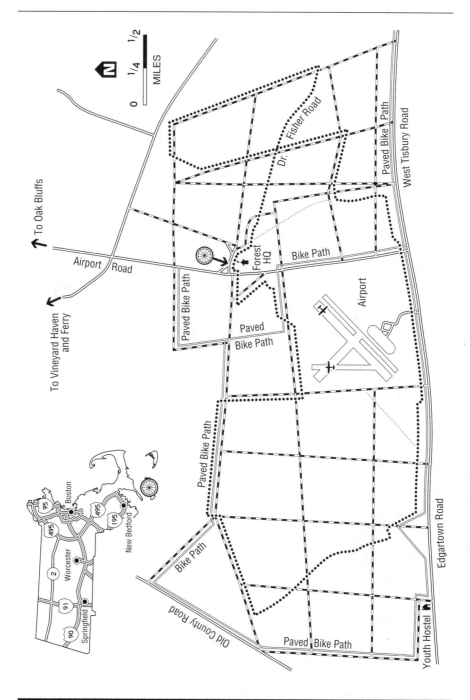

Crossing a secluded field. Martha's Vineyard State Forest, Martha's Vineyard, Massachusetts.

Some of the trails in the state park, however, are published for the first time in this book.

Finding the trail: See the Lagoon Pond—Lake Tashmoo ride (under "Finding the trail" on pages 120–21) for directions on how to reach Martha's Vineyard by ferry. Once you're at the ferry landing in Vineyard Haven, the most pleasant route to the state park uses the beginning of the Lagoon Pond—Lake Tashmoo ride. When you come out on Edgartown Road, turn left. You will reach a blinking light. Turn right on Airport Road; the state park sign and access road come up on the left.

Sources of additional information:

Vineyard Offroad Bicycling Association (VORBA)
(508) 693-4905 or (508) 693-1878
This club holds group rides for all ability levels.

Martha's Vineyard Chamber of Commerce
P.O. Box 1698, Beach Road
Vineyard Haven, MA 02568
(508) 693-0085

Notes on the trail: As long as you stay oriented north-south and east-west, this is an easy ride to follow because the entire forest is crisscrossed with a grid of fire lanes. You begin by riding up the paved access road and forking left (the right road is the ranger's driveway).

The trickiest part of the ride comes now. You go straight through a 4-way intersection, across the first fire lane, and take the second one to the left. You will reach a large field, and pick up a narrow, grassy trail on the left of the field, just behind a tree line. This trail, Dr. Fisher Road, becomes much more obvious. Again, cross a fire lane, and then turn left onto the second one.

Watch for a single-track trail (marked with several rocks on the ground) on the right, after about a half mile. This trail comes out on a fire lane on the border of the park. Turn right, veer to the right on the northeastern corner of the park, pass a fire lane on the right, and watch for a grassy single-track trail crossing the fire lane diagonally. Turn sharply right onto this trail, which is the other side of Dr. Fisher Road. (If you miss this turn, you almost immediately reach another fire lane.)

Ride along this double-track trail to a fire lane, and turn left (this is where you turned left before, from the other direction). Turn right on the next fire lane. You will come out at a large field, with a windmill pumping drinkable water into a bathtub. Just after the field, turn left onto a single-track trail.

Just before you reach the bike path next to a paved road, turn right onto another single-track trail. This trail comes out at a paved road. Make a dogleg turn to the left and right on the pavement, and pick up the bike path along the paved road. Ride past the airport, and just after the airport turn right at a fence onto a trail. You will come out on the bike path again; turn right. When the bike path veers to the left, bear right onto a fire lane. Just after descending over a hill, turn sharply left onto a single-track trail, and bear to the right.

The trail will end at a wide fire lane. Turn right, and you will reach a small clearing with the bike path crossing through it. Pick up the bike path heading in the same direction, cross another fire lane, and turn right (southward) on the next fire lane. You will reach a junction at the northwest corner of the airport. Turn left, pick up the bike path going in the same direction, and then turn left onto a single-track trail just before you reach Airport Road.

This trail comes out at a field. Turn left onto a dirt road on the other side of the field, and you will reach a T junction with another fire road. Turn right and you come out on Airport Road. Cross the road and pick up a trail that soon comes out at the forest headquarters.

CONNECTICUT

Western Connecticut

RIDE 34 *HUNTINGTON STATE PARK*

This undeveloped park has little in it, except for attractive woods, a lake, a pond, a lagoon, and about ten miles of trails looping around. You can take short, easy rides that circumvent bodies of water, or a more challenging tour on longer and more rugged loops that involve some loose terrain and mud. Coming or going from the trailhead, be sure to take the trail along the western border of the park. This route runs through a highland field with a good view.

Along the trails note the many large, handsome bushes with dark green leaves. This is mountain laurel, whose blossoms are the state flower. Keep an eye out also for equestrians—a horse farm borders the park to the north. If you ride near a horse, it's best to stop and let it pass, for some horses are frightened by creatures with human torsos and two-wheeled bodies. Nearby, Putnam Memorial Park also has trails.

General location: The park is about 8 miles southeast of Danbury, in the town of Redding.

Elevation change: The terrain here is relatively flat, but with many short, steep climbs and descents (some of which are made more challenging by loose terrain).

Season: Locals recommend this park as a 4-season ride, but they also suggest not riding here in wet weather.

Services: All services are available in Bethel and Danbury, including two mountain bike shops: Bethel Cycle in Bethel, (203) 792-4640, and Bike Express in Danbury, (203) 792-5460.

Hazards: Watch for loose gravel and heavily eroded areas on some of the descents. Also, yield to horseback riders and watch out for strollers. When approaching walkers or equestrians from behind, announce yourself in plenty of time.

Rescue index: At most you will be about 1 mile from help.

Land status: State park trails.

Maps: A trail map is available from the Bureau of Parks and Forests (see below); you might be able to pick one up at Bethel Cycle in Bethel.

Finding the trail: From CT 15 (the Merritt Parkway), take Exit 45 onto CT 58, heading north toward Redding. After about 8 miles, turn right onto Sunset Hill Road and watch for an unmarked parking area on the left (with 2 stone pillars in it). From the north, take Exit 5 on Interstate 84, onto CT 53 East, toward Danbury. Head south through Danbury on CT 53 (Main Street). After 2.5 miles,

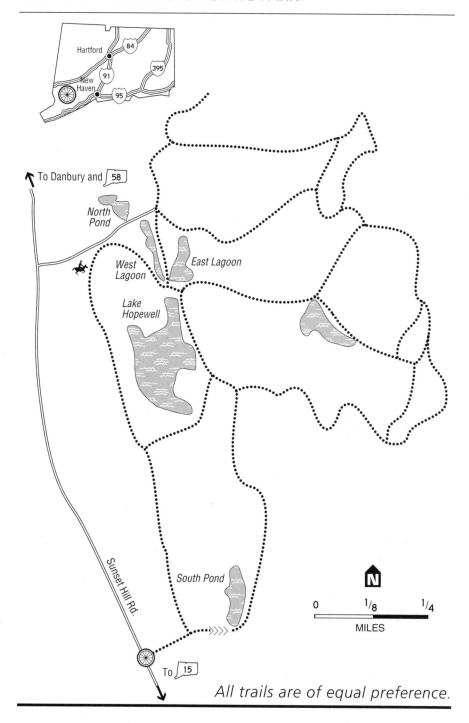

Hartford

New Haven

84

91

395

95

To Danbury and 58

North Pond

West Lagoon

East Lagoon

Lake Hopewell

Sunset Hill Rd.

South Pond

To 15

N

0   1/8   1/4
MILES

All trails are of equal preference.

turn left onto CT 302, then right onto CT 58 South, and left onto Sunset Hill Road. After a couple of miles, you will reach the parking area on the left.

Sources of additional information:

Bureau of Parks and Forests
Department of Environmental Protection
165 Capital Avenue
Hartford, CT 06106
(203) 566-2305

Notes on the trail: You can take many different rides in this park by connecting different loops. For a scenic, less steep beginning, turn left at the trailhead and cruise through an open field, then veer right and descend into the woods. (The trail heading straight down from the parking area is steep and eroded.) To familiarize yourself with the park, you might first circumvent the 3 ponds and then explore longer, more secluded loops to the east.

RIDE 35 *TRUMBULL / OLD MINE PARK*

This moderate nine-mile loop connects three different trails: a 3.5-mile rail-trail, a 1.5-mile loop around an old mine (now a park), and a more challenging 2.5-mile single-track along a river. Each section can be done separately.

The flat, wooded double-track rail-trail runs next to a gorge with a lively river tumbling down it. At the northern end of this former railroad bed you reach Old Mine Park, a popular recreation area, with fields and a rugged loose-gravel trail looping past an old mining site.

Then, after riding on pavement for a mile or so, you will reach the other side of the river, where there's another park. This one has a BMX race track in it, which you might enjoy trying out. Then it's into deep pine woods on a single-track trail along the river's edge. This rugged trail passes over roots and rocks, across a stream, through a former reservoir (drained in 1935), and across the river itself.

General location: The river valley is just north of the town of Trumbull, off CT 25.
Elevation change: The terrain is flat, except for a short, steep climb on a loose-gravel jeep road (in Old Mine Park) and a steep descent on pavement.
Season: Any time between late spring and late fall is good for riding here.
Services: All services are available on CT 127 and in Trumbull.
Hazards: To complete this loop you must walk across the river for about 30 feet in shallow water. Also, be ready to switch riding techniques when moving

RIDE 35 *TRUMBULL*

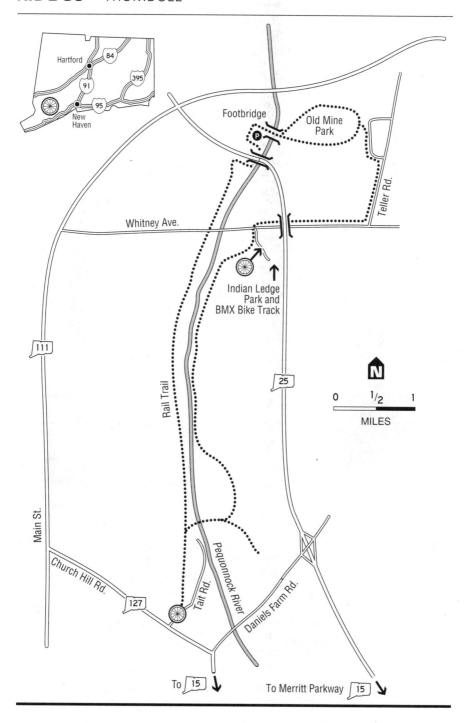

A scenic rail-trail. Trumbull, Connecticut.

from flat, smooth trails to pavement, then to technical single-track. Watch out for traffic on a highway that you must cross after a steep descent (just before Indian Ledge Park).

Rescue index: At most you will be about a quarter-mile from help.

Land status: Public trails and a former railroad bed. The river valley was purchased for public use in 1987 for $9.2 million.

Maps: The parks and cross streets will appear on a detailed state map. The trails are easy to follow.

Finding the trail: From CT 15 (the Merritt Parkway), take the Trumbull/Route 127 exit and head north toward Trumbull on White Plains Road. After 1.3 miles, just after crossing CT 25, turn right onto Tait Road. After a few hundred feet, you will see the trail forking uphill on the left, behind some boulders. Park off the road, and be sure to lock your vehicle. From CT 25, take Exit 9 onto Daniels Farm Road. At the light in Trumbull, turn right onto Tait Road. You can also begin riding from the parking lot at Old Mine Park at the northern end of the ride.

Sources of additional information: The *Hometown Publications* newspaper has published a historical guidebook for this area. Copies may be obtained by writing to: Hometown Publications, P.O. Box 298, Trumbull, CT 06611.

Notes on the trail: After about 1 mile on the rail-trail (which was part of the Housatonic Railroad until 1932), you will pass a double-track trail forking down to the right, toward the river. This is where the loop comes out. You might want to ride down and check out the depth of the water, since you will be crossing it later. For a technical ride, take this fork, cross the river, and head north on the single-track. Otherwise, after about 2.5 miles on the rail-trail, you will cross paved Whitney Avenue. Shortly afterward, you pass Parlor Rock Park, the site of an amusement park in the nineteenth century. Today, alas, there remain only trees and a plaque.

Now comes the tricky junction. Just before reaching CT 25, a highway, fork off the rail-trail onto a single-track trail on the right. Stay in the woods, riding along the highway, and soon veer left underneath the highway bridge, then left again, and onto a trail that parallels the highway. The trail widens into the rail-trail again, and comes out at a paved parking area at Old Mine Park. Cross the footbridge onto the grassy area and ride into the woods on a loose-gravel jeep road.

You can loop around this trail, and then fork off it on the east side, onto a trail that soon reaches a paved road. Turn right on the pavement, right onto paved Skating Pond Road, and right again onto paved Teller Road. After a steep downhill, you will reach a T junction at paved Whitney Avenue.

Turn right, ride under CT 25, and turn left almost immediately onto a paved road with a sign at it for Indian Ledge Park. You can ride on this access road to a BMX racetrack. Otherwise, soon after turning off CT 25, look for a large metal gate on the right, with a trail behind it that heads south along the river. Follow this single-track trail, staying close to the river. After a couple of miles, you will reach a large clearing on the left; this is a former reservoir basin. Ride a quarter of the way around the clearing counterclockwise and pick up a double-track trail heading south again. You will reach a fork just before the river. Turn right, descend to the river (see Hazards), and pick up the rail-trail on the other side. Turn left to reach the trailhead.

RIDE 36 *STEEP ROCK RESERVATION*

It's worth a trip to pastoral Washington County to enjoy this large, secluded reservation with 20 to 30 miles of trails and unpaved roads. There's terrain here for all levels of riders. Novices can cruise on interconnecting dirt roads, a rail-trail that passes through a granite tunnel, and a path along the Shepaug River. More experienced riders will want to tackle the rugged, steep single-track trails. One trail leads to a lookout with a view of the entire park.

The reservation was created in the 1880s by a local conservationist who gave the town of Washington "a tract of land known as 'Steep Rock' partly improved by paths for foot travel and by roads for use by horses and horse-drawn vehicles." Today, the site is managed by the Steep Rock Association, a private trusteeship that describes the area as: "an incomparably lovely tract of land, with a river winding through its valley and the precipitous hills on either side—all interlaced with riding and hiking trails, with noble trees overhanging and here and there on the ridges, a beautiful vista of the valley and the river and the higher hills beyond." The reservation is also popular for swimming, canoeing, and fishing.

General location: This reservation is just outside the town of Washington Depot.
Elevation change: The terrain is flat along the river, but has steep climbs with rugged terrain and lots of switchbacks on perimeter trails.
Season: Avoid riding here in the spring because of mud.
Services: All services are available in Washington Depot and the Bike Express in New Milford, (203) 354-1466.
Hazards: Watch for logs and other hidden obstructions in the fall and winter. Also, ride slowly or stop when passing horseback riders and other park users. Remember, this is a multi-use park.
Rescue index: The dirt roads are patrolled by rangers and the area is surrounded by homes.
Land status: The trails and roads are managed by a private trusteeship that maintains this area for the "use and enjoyment of citizens and residents of Washington and Litchfield County and of their guests and friends and of the general public."
Maps: A trail map published by the Steep Rock Association is available for a modest charge at the Hickory Stick Book Shop in Washington Depot, (203) 868-0525, or directly from the Steep Rock Association for $1 (see below).
Finding the trail: From the center of Washington Depot, take the road across from the Hickory Stick Book Shop and next to the Mobil Station. Veer right, and after 1.5 miles you will reach the parking area at the reservation.

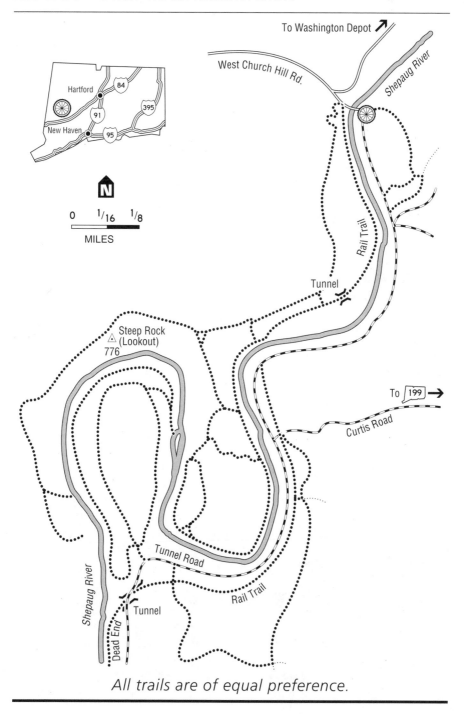

To Washington Depot

West Church Hill Rd.

Shepaug River

Hartford

84

91

395

New Haven

95

N

0   1/16   1/8
MILES

Rail Trail

Tunnel

Steep Rock
△ (Lookout)
776

To 199 →

Curtis Road

Tunnel Road

Shepaug River

Rail Trail

Tunnel

Dead End

All trails are of equal preference.

Sources of additional information:

Steep Rock Association
P.O. Box 279
Washington Depot, CT 06794
(203) 868-9131

Bike Express
73A Bridge Street
New Milford, CT 06776
(203) 354-1466

Notes on the trail: It's easy to orient yourself by the river that runs lengthwise through the reservation. Almost all trails loop back to it. You can begin riding on either side of the river and bridge at the parking lot. More challenging trails run along the perimeter of the reservation, farther away from the river. Perimeter trails to the east have some especially tough hills, and there's plenty of climbing toward the lookout, too. Easier trails are closer to the river.

RIDE 37 *TOUR DE CANTON*

This 17-mile loop ride climbs on a rugged double-track trail through a hardwood forest, descends through a historic town, cruises around a secluded reservoir area, tackles some old roads in a state forest, and parallels a white-water river on an unpaved road. Although the tour can be managed by beginning mountain bikers, its length and extended climbs make it more suited to intermediate riders. Experts will be able to complete it in about an hour and a half.

After climbing past oaks and birches for about 1.5 miles, the ride descends on pavement through picturesque Collinsville. Next, you cruise on a secluded old asphalt road past the Nepaug Reservoir for several miles. Then it's on to double-track trails for several miles through light woods, before you enter Nepaug State Forest. (There you can ride on miles of single-track trails—see Ride 38.) You pick up a rugged four-wheel-drive road that comes out at the lively Farmington River, which is a favorite spot for swimming and tubing. Finally, it's a cruise for a couple of miles along paved US 202 into Canton.

General location: The ride begins and ends in Canton, and winds around the Nepaug Reservoir to the west of Canton.
Elevation change: There's a fair amount of climbing on this ride. It begins at 350', climbs to 700', descends to 300', climbs steadily over several miles to 900', and then descends for several miles to 350', for a total elevation gain of 1,900'.
Season: This is a good 4-season ride, if there is little snow.

RIDE 37 *TOUR DE CANTON*

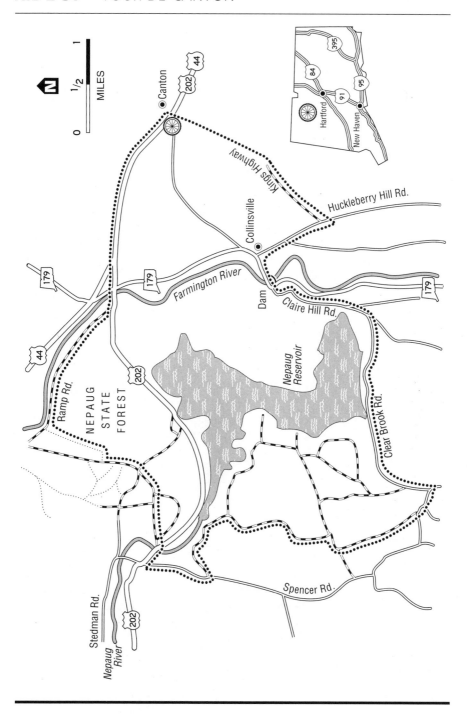

Touring on a double-track trail. Canton, Connecticut.

Services: All services are available in Canton, including Summit Mountain Bike on US 44, (203) 693-8891, which has a lot of information about mountain biking in this area. The shop also sponsors regular group rides.

Hazards: Watch for traffic on the active roads, especially on the steep descent on pavement into Collinsville (near the beginning of the ride) and on US 44 at the end of the ride.

Rescue index: At most, you will be about a half mile from help.

Land status: Active town roads, old public roads, and old roads and trails in a state forest.

Maps: A detailed state road map will show the active roads on this ride; this map fills in the rest.

Finding the trail: The ride begins on US 44 at the village green in the center of Canton. You can park next to the green or on side streets.

Sources of additional information:

Summit Mountain Bike
US 44
Canton, CT 06019
(203) 693-8891

Notes on the trail: Behind the village green, ride up Canton Springs Road until it ends at an old farm site, where it becomes a double-track trail. Climb steeply for a half mile on this rocky trail and then descend. The trail turns into a dirt road, then a paved road, and comes out on paved Huckleberry Hill Road. Turn right and descend steeply into Collinsville, turn left onto Main Street, and left again onto Bridge Street. Cross the Farmington River and climb up the steep paved road on the other side of the bridge.

At the top of the hill, turn left onto Claire Hill Road. Fork left onto Barnes Hill Road, and then left again onto Clear Brook Road, which runs along the southern edge of the reservoir. After about 2 miles on this secluded road, turn right up the first paved road, fork right at the top of the hill, and look for blue blazes on a trail on the right. Turn right onto this trail. At the next several turns, follow the white signs for the "Tunxis Trail." When you come out on dirt Valentin Road, turn right, and pick up the double-track on the left (again at a sign for the Tunxis Trail). Keep following the Tunxis Trail signs.

You will come out onto paved Spencer Road. Turn right, ride to the intersection with US 202, turn right, and watch for the forest sign on the left at an unpaved access road into Nepaug State Forest. Turn left, ride up the access road a short distance, and fork right. Turn right at the next intersection and you'll reach a 6-way intersection (4 roads and a power line trail). Turn sharply right, reach a 4-way intersection, and turn left onto Satan's Kingdom Road. On a downhill, watch for a blue-blazed trail on the right behind 5 large boulders. Turn right there, descend, and turn left at the bottom onto an overgrown old road.

You will come out on two-wheel-drive Ramp Road along the Farmington River. Turn right, come out on a paved road, and turn right to reach US 202. Turn left, then go straight through an intersection with CT 179, and ride on the shoulder of US 202/US 44 into Canton.

RIDE 38 *NEPAUG STATE FOREST*

Here's a small, secluded forest (1,100 acres) that's packed with single-track trails and narrow dirt roads. Local mountain bikers maintain a moderately challenging five-mile loop here on single-track trails and old dirt roads. Or you can take an easier ride by sticking to the roads.

Another favorite local ride in this forest takes the Tunxis Trail northward to Satans Kingdom and a lookout to the west. You can also extend this ride by forking off the Tunxis Trail at the northern end of the loop, onto other twisting trails, including a fun descent to the river.

With its sandy ground and abundance of pine trees, the terrain here looks like it could be nearer the seacoast. There's good swimming on the Farmington River at the end of Satans Kingdom Road. This is also a favorite site for river tubing.

General location: Near the town of New Hartford, 4.5 miles west of Canton and 20 miles west of Hartford.

Elevation change: This ride rolls up and down between 550' and 700', alternating between short, steep ascents and descents and longer, more gradual ones.

Season: Any time between late spring and late fall is good for riding. Winter is fine, too, if there's no snow.

Services: All services are available in Canton, including the Summit Mountain Bike Shop on US 44, (203) 693-8891, which is a meeting spot for mountain bikers. Group rides leave this bike shop on Saturday mornings.

Hazards: Watch for obstructions on the tighter single-track trails and soft spots on the sand-surfaced roads.

Rescue index: At most you will be about 1.5 miles from a traveled road.

Land status: An active town road and old roads and trails in a state forest.

Maps: Summit Mountain Bike in Canton carries a hand-drawn map of this ride. You can also contact the Bureau of Parks and Forests (see below).

Finding the trail: From the junction of US 202 and US 44, just west of Canton, head west on US 202. At 2.8 miles, turn right onto a narrow, unpaved road with a half-hidden brown sign: "Nepaug State Forest." A few hundred feet up the road, park at turnoffs under the pine trees.

Sources of additional information:

Summit Mountain Bike
US 44
Canton, CT 06019
(203) 693-8891

Bureau of Parks and Forests
Department of Environmental Protection

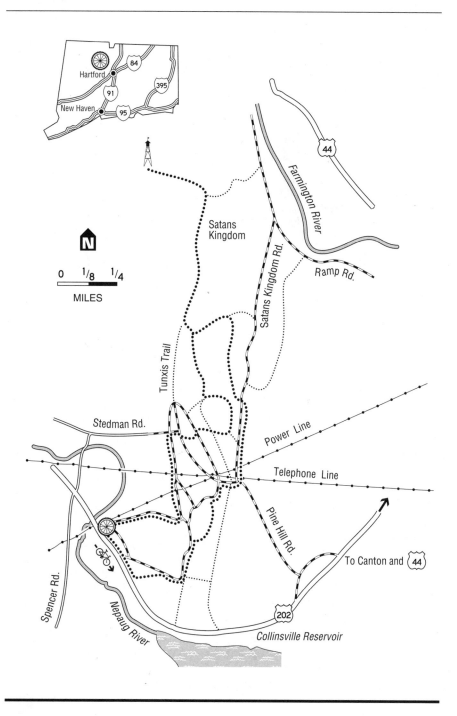

Fast cruising on hard-packed sand. Nepaug State Forest, New Hartford, Connecticut.

165 Capital Avenue
Hartford, CT 06106
(203) 566-2305

Notes on the trail: There are many turns on this compact 5-mile loop. Local mountain bikers, who maintain this ride, hope in the future to mark it with colored blazes. Until then, you might familiarize yourself with the layout of the forest by using the several dirt roads that interconnect in it.

To ride the entire loop, begin by forking immediately onto a single-track trail on the right side of the dirt road at the trailhead. You will reach the dirt road after less than a half mile. Turn right on it and, on a downhill, fork right into the woods. You will come out at a jeep road and turn left on it (heading north). At a 3-way intersection with an island, dogleg right and left, and cross a power line. You're now on Satans Kingdom Road.

A tricky turn: You must watch for a single-track trail heading into the woods on the left, up an embankment. Take it, fork right almost immediately, and then dogleg left and right on the trail. You will reach a logging clearing and will turn left uphill. You will join another wider trail. This is the Tunxis Trail. You can turn right on it to reach a lookout. Or veer left and, after a downhill, you will reach a gate and continue straight ahead. At a 4-way intersection, turn left. After a few hundred feet, fork left. You will reach a T junction and turn right. After a downhill, you will reach a 3-way intersection at a clearing and turn right again. Cross a dirt road and you will reach another road; turn right on it. Follow this road back toward the trailhead.

RIDE 39 *WEST HARTFORD RESERVOIR*

This challenging eight-mile loop ride explores a favorite place for mountain biking just outside Hartford, the state capital. In fact, on almost any weekend the parking lot here looks like there might be a mountain biking convention in progress. The heart of the ride runs for several miles along the famous Metacomet Trail. You will return on other single-track trails. You can also take an easier route, using secluded dirt roads.

Single- and double-track trails make up most of this ride, with a few stretches on woods roads. From the well-maintained reservoir area, it's a climb to a wooded ridge, then a side trail to a lookout. *Note:* The paved roads skirting the reservoirs are popular walking loops. The Metropolitan District Commission, which manages the area, has requested that cyclists avoid riding on them. In other words, head for the hills.

General location: The reservoir is about 8 miles west of Hartford.
Elevation change: The ride begins with a fairly steep climb of about 400'. Afterward, you'll cruise along a ridge and then descend gradually.
Season: This is a 4-season ride, but expect mud in the spring.
Services: All services are available along CT 4 and in West Hartford. Summit Mountain Bikes in Canton, about 10 miles to the northwest, has a lot of information about mountain biking areas and group rides.
Hazards: Watch for occasional obstructions on the single-track trails. Also, avoid startling walkers by announcing yourself when passing from behind.
Rescue index: At most you will be about 1 mile from help.
Land status: You will be pedaling Metropolitan District Commission (MDC) trails, the blue-blazed Metacomet Trail, and woods roads, all open for biking at the discretion of the Commission.

Blue-blazed trails, which are found throughout Connecticut, are not officially open for mountain biking; access is determined by local park rangers. In this area, rangers actually prefer that cyclists use the trails rather than the paved roads around the reservoirs.

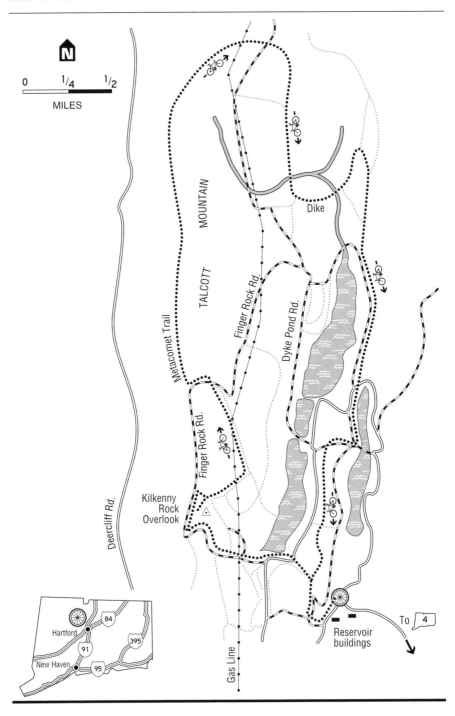

N

0   1/4   1/2

MILES

MOUNTAIN

TALCOTT

Metacomet Trail

Finger Rock Rd.

Dike

Dyke Pond Rd.

Finger Rock Rd.

Deercliff Rd.

Kilkenny
Rock
Overlook

Hartford

84

395

91

New Haven

95

Gas Line

To 4

Reservoir
buildings

Coming out of the woods. West Hartford, Connecticut.

Maps: You can buy a good trail map for $2 at the trailhead in the Filter Plant Administration Building, which is the nearest building to CT.4. A copy of this map is also posted on a board in the main parking lot.

Finding the trail: From CT 4 in West Hartford, turn right into the reservoir area at two large stone pillars and a large sign saying, "West Hartford Water Treatment Plant." Fork right on the access road, pass several buildings, and you will reach a large parking area.

Sources of additional information: Mountain bikers are always coming and going in the main parking lot. Ask them about other riding possibilities, or hook up with a riding partner.

Summit Mountain Bikes
US 44/202
Canton, CT 06019
(203) 693-8891

Notes on the trail: Because there are some long, secluded trails and woods roads in this area, it's a good idea to buy a trail map at the administration building (see "Maps"). You might also carry a compass.

To reach the ridge, head south from the parking area on a paved road and, within a few hundred feet, fork right onto a double-track trail just across from a reservoir. Then turn sharply right onto a dirt road, and soon fork left onto a narrower trail, and then fork left again. When you reach a clearing, turn right up a short, steep hill, and you will reach a paved road around a reservoir.

Turn left (counterclockwise) on the road and, at the next intersection, go straight uphill. After a half mile or so, turn right onto a rugged road. (For an easier ride, continue on this road, Finger Rock Road.) Soon veer right onto a trail and climb to a lookout (Kilkenny Rock).

Next, descend back to the jeep road and turn right, soon reaching a gas pipeline trail. Turn left on the gas pipeline trail and almost immediately right, crossing the gas pipeline and forking left onto a trail that parallels the gas line (the right fork leads to another view). You will cross the gas line again, and then turn left onto a dirt road at a T junction. Turn sharply right at a fork, onto another dirt road. At a wide clearing at a power line, fork left onto a single-track trail. This is the blue-blazed Metacomet Trail, a major north-south trail.

You will cross the gas line again (about 5 miles into the ride, now heading west to east). Then you will soon cross a paved road, staying on the cleared trail, and fork right (south) at the next turn. (You can reach more trails toward Talcott Mountain to the north by turning left on the road.) Then veer to the left, and you will reach a fork at a large clearing.

At this point both trails head south. One option is to veer left across the clearing and a flood control dike. After a couple of mudholes, turn right onto a single-track trail. (If you miss this turn, you will reach a field and US 44.) At a 4-way intersection with a fence on the other side, turn right. Then turn left onto a dirt road, follow it to a paved road, fork left, and turn right on another paved road. Almost immediately, turn right onto a narrower road, and then left onto a trail going south. Veer to the left onto a wider road and you're heading back to the parking area.

RIDE 40   *PENNWOOD STATE PARK*

Single-track riding doesn't get much better than the northern part of this ride, which is a narrow, moderately challenging trail winding along a mountain ridge and offering panoramic views. This 10-mile route combines this fun, scenic out-and-back trail with more paths to the south of it.

You can take an easier ride by staying on a narrow old asphalt "trail" from the parking area and an out-and-back double-track trail, or challenge yourself by opting instead for a couple of highly technical single-track trails (see "Notes on the trail").

Whichever you prefer, it's fun (and occasionally hair-raising) to try keeping up with the local racers-in-training, who congregate at this popular site.

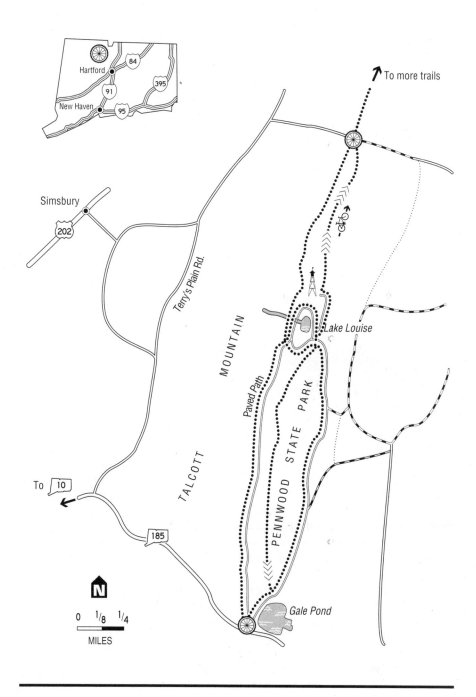

General location: The park is located 9 miles or so northwest of Hartford, on CT 185.

Elevation change: You begin at about 425', climb gradually and steadily to 550', and then descend.

Season: This is a 4-season ride, if there is little snow. There is good drainage in wet weather.

Services: All services are available along US 44, including Summit Mountain Bike, (203) 693-8891, in Canton, which has information about mountain biking in this area and holds group rides. There's also The Bicycle Cellar on Hop Meadow Street in Simsbury, (203) 658-1311, and Bloomfield Bicycle and Repair on Seneca Road in Bloomfield, (203) 242-9884.

Hazards: Less-experienced riders should not attempt to "clean" all obstacles on the single-track trails. Know your limits.

Rescue index: You will be about 2 miles from help on well-used trails.

Land status: Trails in a state park.

Maps: USGS, 7.5 minute series, Avon, CT.

Finding the trail: On CT 185, about 8 miles west of Hartford and about 2 miles east of CT 10, watch for signs on the north for Pennwood State Park. Turn into the paved parking lot, which is just off CT 185.

Sources of additional information:

Bureau of Parks and Forests
Department of Environmental Protection
165 Capital Avenue
Hartford, CT 06106
(203) 566-2305

Summit Mountain Bike
US 44
Canton, CT 06019
(203) 693-8891

Notes on the trail: Pick up a narrow asphalt "trail" on the north side of the parking lot. Climb on it, and after about 2 miles you will see a long wooden bridge in the woods on the left. You now can reach an unpaved single-track trail heading north either by turning left, crossing the bridge and turning right, or by continuing on the asphalt trail, forking left, and reaching a wide area with a sign: "Pennwood Nature Trail." A trail forking north from this area connects with the main north-south trail.

For a fun, occasionally death-defying single-track ride, continue climbing on the asphalt trail for a short distance and pick up a trail at the top that passes a lookout on the left, then becomes a tight, steep trail for 1.5 miles.

Both trails come out at a cul-de-sac on a paved road. (Some local riders prefer to begin at this point.) Cross the pavement and pick up a single-track trail, fork left almost immediately, and ride north for several more miles, passing several

Board riding. Pennwood State Park, Simsbury, Connecticut.

lookouts. Then double back to the dead-end paved road and pick up the double-track trail on the right. (The more difficult single-track trail on the left is not rideable southward.)

When you reach the paved loop again, you have 3 choices to return to the parking lot: descend on the same narrow asphalt trail you climbed on, loop around on the wider half of the asphalt trail (which becomes a road), or pick up a technical single-track trail on the southern side of the 3-way intersection at the Pennwood Nature Trail sign.

RIDE 41 *WESTWOODS*

This 2,000-acre woods near the Atlantic Ocean has more than 20 miles of single-track trails. A few trails are easy, many are moderate, and more than a few rank as quite difficult. You can do an easy out-and-back ride on flat trails, or a challenging 15-mile loop on rugged single-track.

This site is a favorite spot for hiking, horseback riding, and bird-watching. Its tight network of trails is therefore best explored at a moderate pace. Less experienced cyclists might take the Blue Trail (east-west) and the Green and Orange trails (north-south). More advanced riders will want to tackle some of the narrower, steeper crossover trails. A few trails pass through marshland, making them wet year-round. Because this is a popular site, the trails are fairly well maintained—but sometimes more for hiking than biking.

This area is full of ecological niches. You'll enjoy marshes, hemlock forests, stands of hardwood trees, deep green mountain laurel bushes, and wildflowers such as trailing arbutus. As noted on a trail map in the *Connecticut Walk Book* (see "Maps"), there are over a dozen scenic sites here: vistas, prehistoric rock carvings (petroglyphs), a waterfall, and giant rock formations called "glacial erratics." On the southern side of paved CT 146, the White Trail runs along a saltwater marsh—a rare opportunity to mountain bike near the ocean.

General location: These woods are located in Guilford, near the junction of Interstate 95 and US 1, 10 miles east of New Haven and Interstate 91.
Elevation change: The terrain is relatively flat, with some short, steep climbs.
Season: Any time except spring or after a rainfall is good for riding in this occasionally marshy area.
Services: All services are available in Guilford and along US 1.
Hazards: Despite its compactness and proximity to the seashore, these woods contain some technical trails. Beginners should expect to walk in places if they explore some trails; even more experienced riders must keep an eye out for hidden or sudden obstructions. Also, riders must slow down or stop for occasional hikers and horseback riders.
Rescue index: At most you will be about 1 mile from a traveled road.
Land status: Trails in public woods.
Maps: A detailed trail map is found in the *Connecticut Walk Book,* a well-known hiking book available in many outdoor stores or by mail from the Connecticut Forest and Parks Association, a private, non-profit organization (see below) for $17.
Finding the trail: On I-95, take Exit 57, turning right onto US 1 toward Guilford. After less than a mile, across from Bishop's Orchard and fruit stand on the

RIDE 41 *WESTWOODS*

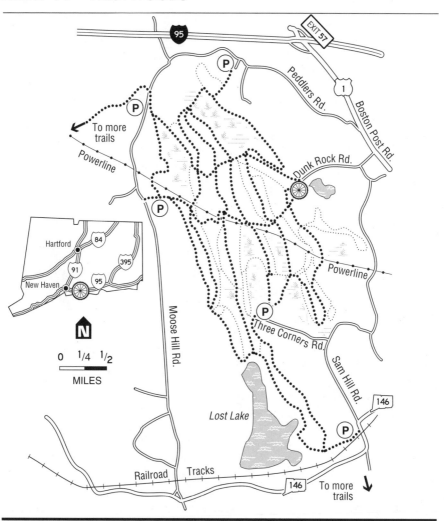

left, turn right onto Dunk Rock Road, which dead-ends at a parking area next to a field.

Sources of additional information:

Connecticut Forest and Parks Association
16 Meriden Road
Rockfall, CT 06481
(203) 346-2372

A half-hidden trail. Westwoods, Guilford, Connecticut.

Notes on the trail: This compact area is laced with trails, each blazed in a different color. The map here shows only the major trails. Many routes are blazed in more than one color, however, since each functions as a hiking trail, horseback trail, and a crossover trail. A few guidelines:

- Respect the rhythms of other trail users.
- The Blue Trail is the main east-west trail.
- The Green, Orange, White, and Yellow trails run north-south.
- The Green and Orange trails are the easiest; the White Trail is more difficult; the Yellow Trail is the most difficult.

- Major routes are blazed with colored circles, while hiking trails are marked by triangles.
- A power line intersects the area from east to west; you can use it to orient yourself.
- Take the White Trail south across CT 146 to reach a tidal marsh area.

RIDE 42 *WADSWORTH FALLS STATE PARK*

This well-used park has about six miles of fun single-track trails that interconnect in loops ranging from easy to challenging. Easier trails in the northern section of the park wind through a handsome forest of hemlock, basswood, beech, and birch trees. To do a more challenging four-mile perimeter loop, take the rugged Laurel Brook Trail, the White Birch Trail, Cedar Loop Trail, and the Main Trail down to the railroad tracks. From there, a trail goes past dramatic Wadsworth Falls.

This former estate has both man-made and natural highlights. These include a stone house foundation and stone bridge, 200-year-old trees, a mammoth mountain laurel on the Main Trail (marked by a plaque), and wide, 50-foot-high Wadsworth Falls on the Coginchaug River. There's also swimming and picnicking in the park. For intellectual exercise, there's nearby Wesleyan University in Middletown, known for its world-class cultural offerings. *Note:* The park is also used by hikers from nearby cities.

General location: The park is in Middlefield, 3 miles southwest of Middletown.
Elevation change: Some of these trails have regular short, steep climbs and descents.
Season: This is a 3-season ride: summer, fall, and winter. Local riders recommend staying off the trails in March and April because of wetness. Also, one must be aware of other trail users, especially on sunny weekends in summer and fall.
Services: Water and restrooms are located at the parking lot; all other services are in Middletown and along CT 66.
Hazards: Watch out for some narrow, eroded areas along steep banks on the Laurel Brook Trail. And watch out for other park users.
Rescue index: At most you will be about a half mile from help.
Land status: State park trails.
Maps: Trail maps are usually stocked at the parking lot. You can also contact the Bureau of Parks and Forests (see below).
Finding the trail: From CT 9 take Exit 15 toward CT 66 and Wesleyan University. Pass through Middletown on CT 66 and turn left onto CT 157. Follow signs for the park, which comes up on the right.

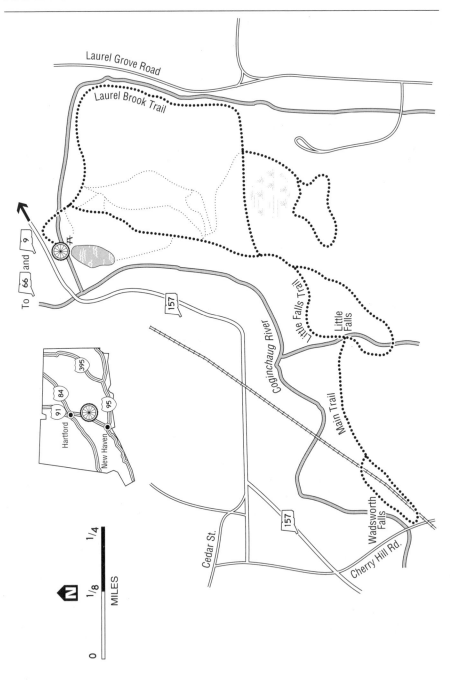

Checking out a sign at the trailhead. Wadsworth Falls State Park, Middlefield, Connecticut.

Sources of additional information:

> Bureau of Parks and Forests
> Department of Environmental Protection
> 165 Capital Avenue
> Hartford, CT 06106
> (203) 566-2305

Notes on the trail: Most of the trails in this park are blazed in different colors. To take the 4-mile perimeter loop, begin by turning left at the first fork, heading away from the parking lot onto the Bridge Trail. Then circumvent the park on the Laurel Brook Trail, White Birch Trail, Cedar Loop Trail, and Main Trail heading southwest. Turn right onto paved Cherry Hill Road, cross the tracks, and pick up a trail on the left edge of the tracks, soon veering left into the woods. The trail passes by Wadsworth Falls.

Continue on this single-track trail until it comes out at the railroad tracks again. Cross the railroad bed and pick up the trail on the other side, veering right immediately and then left onto the Main Trail.

For a technical ride, turn left onto the Little Falls Trail, which comes out on the Main Trail. Follow the Main Trail back to the parking area.

Eastern Connecticut

RIDE 43 COCKAPONSET STATE FOREST

You can ride all day in this 15,000-acre forest that is crisscrossed by at least 20 miles of trails and several unpaved roads. This challenging ten-mile loop ride heads north from Pattaconk Lake, a local recreational area, on technical single-track trails. Then it switches to a two-wheel-drive dirt road, a double-track trail, a jeep road, and more single-track trails. You can loop back on old asphalt Filley Road, or take dirt roads and trails that fan off it.

This second-largest state forest in Connecticut, named after a Native American chief, is a huge woodscape of broadleaf trees (oaks, maples, and dogwoods), dark green pines, and mountain laurel bushes. The Pattaconk Lake Recreation Area at the trailhead is a popular site for swimming, sunbathing, and picnicking.

General location: The forest lies in the towns of Haddam and Chester, just off CT 9 and 12 miles south of Middletown.

Elevation change: You will do some steady, not-too-steep climbing on dirt roads and short, steeper rolling on single-track trails.

Season: Any time between late spring and late fall is good for riding in this forest.

Services: All services are available in Middletown. There are several campgrounds in the forest.

Hazards: Watch for minor obstructions on the single-track trails—debris, rocks, and logs. On the two-wheel-drive roads, watch for the occasional vehicle, especially on summer and fall weekends.

Rescue index: At most you will be about 2 miles from help.

Land status: State forest trails and roads.

Maps: Trail maps may be available at forest headquarters, located at the northern border of the forest, off Exit 8 on CT 9. You can also contact the Bureau of Parks and Forests in the Department of Environmental Protection (see below). Many smaller trails are not shown on the official map.

Finding the trail: Take Exit 6 on CT 9, onto CT 148 West. After about 1.5 miles, watch for a large lake next to the highway on the right. Turn right just after it, onto Cedar Lake Road. After another 1.5 miles, make a sharp left turn at a sign for Pattaconk Lake. Pass the lake on the right and you will reach a large parking area on the right.

RIDE 43 COCKAPONSET STATE FOREST

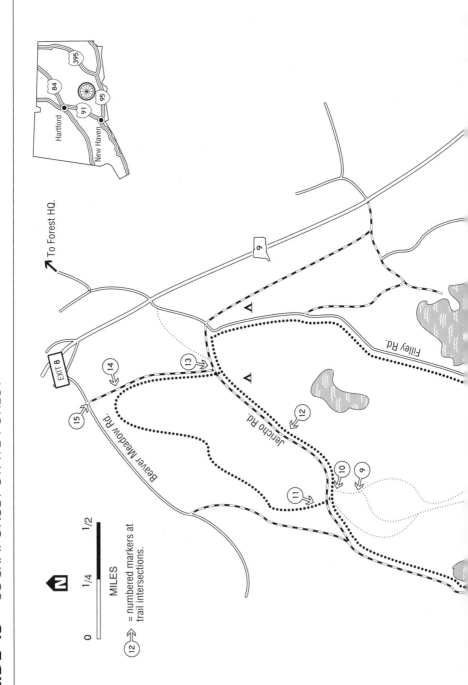

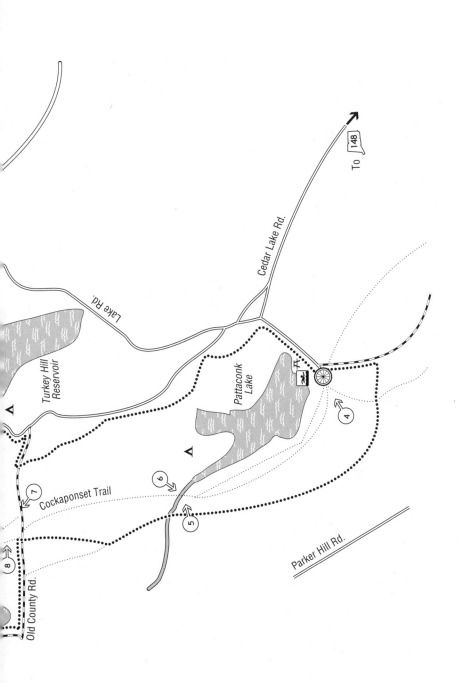

Turkey Hill Reservoir

Lake Rd.

Cedar Lake Rd.

To 148

Pattaconk Lake

Cockaponset Trail

Parker Hill Rd.

Old County Rd.

4

5

6

7

8

Just enough of a trail. Cockaponset State Forest, Haddam, Connecticut.

Sources of additional information:

Bureau of Parks and Forests
Department of Environmental Protection
165 Capital Avenue
Hartford, CT 06106
(203) 566-2305

Notes on the trail: During peak hiking days (sunny weekends in the summer and fall), avoid riding on the blue-blazed Cockaponset Trail and the red-dotted Pattaconk Trail, especially around Pattaconk Lake. Blue-blazed trails in Connecticut are not officially open for mountain biking. However, this policy is modifiable by local park managers. If you're unsure whether or not to ride on a blue-blazed trail, ask a local ranger.

To head north, first ride south for a short distance on Filley Road and turn right onto the first dirt road. Watch for a worn double-track trail on the right. This trail heads north, paralleling the blue-blazed Cockaponset and Pattaconk trails. After about 2 miles, you will intersect unpaved Old County Road. Turn left on it, pass a pond on the right and, immediately after the pond, turn right on a jeep road. When this four-wheel-drive path intersects a two-wheel-drive road, turn right onto this unpaved road, Jericho Road.

Now you can loop northward on one of several trails that fork off Jericho

Road to the north, and then loop back toward the road. Then head south on patchy but smooth-textured asphalt Filley Road. You can turn off this road to the left toward scenic Turkey Hill Reservoir or pick up Old County Road again on the right, and turn onto double- and single-track trails heading south. Farther down Filley Road, several more trails fork off on the right, heading toward Pattaconk Lake.

RIDE 44 *MESHOMASIC STATE FOREST*

This moderately challenging ten-mile loop ride starts on rugged single-track trails for several miles, picks up a jeep road, and finishes on two-wheel-drive dirt roads. The trails require some technical skill, and the dirt roads will test your climbing ability, but neither terrain is too demanding. For less technical riding, you can explore only the dirt roads, which crisscross this oldest state forest (1903) in Connecticut.

On the secluded single-track trails you will be immersed in deep woods, with mature hardwood trees (ash, beech, and maple) and bushes brushing up against your body as you pedal by. From the paved access road (Clark Hill Road), you can reach Great Hill Pond, a local scenic spot. The pond has a foot trail around it that climbs to Great Hill Lookout, a granite outcropping.

General location: This forest is 8 miles east of Middletown, just off CT 2.
Elevation change: The ride has a short, steep climb at the beginning and then regular climbing and descending, with shorter climbs on the trails and longer ones on the roads.
Season: Any time between late spring and late fall is good for riding here. Expect some mud in the spring and after a rainfall.
Services: All services are available in Middletown, 8 miles to the west.
Hazards: Watch out for minor obstructions on the trails and an occasional vehicle on the roads.
Rescue index: At most you will be about 2.5 miles from help.
Land status: State forest roads and trails.
Maps: The *Connecticut Walk Book*, now in its 17th edition, has a map of the trails in this forest and crossroads (not all trails in the book are open for biking, though). The book is available for $17 from the Connecticut Forest and Parks Association, a private, non-profit organization (16 Meriden Road, Rockfall, CT 06481, (203) 346-2372). Some of the trails on this ride are not published anywhere except in this mountain bike book.
Finding the trail: On CT 2, take Exit 13 onto CT 66 toward East Hampton. In East Hampton turn right onto North Main Street and, after just under a mile, turn left onto Clark Hill Road. After 1.5 miles, turn right onto a two-wheel-drive

Expert riders pacing each other. Meshomasic State Forest, East Hampton, Connecticut.

dirt road with a state forest sign at it. After about a half mile, you will reach a parking area on the right, where a blue-dashed trail crosses the road.

Sources of additional information:

Bureau of Parks and Forests
Department of Environmental Protection
165 Capital Avenue
Hartford, CT 06106
(203) 566-2305

Notes on the trail: The first half of this ride weaves on and off the blue-dashed Shenipsit Trail. It is possible to stay on this well-marked trail, but it's not as scenic or as much fun. To orient yourself in the woods, keep heading north for the first 4 miles.

From the parking area, ride back down the road you came up for less than a half mile and turn left onto a double-track trail into the woods. Fork right after a half mile, picking up the blue-dashed trail. Then fork right off the blue-dashed trail onto another trail (at just under a mile from the beginning of the ride).

RIDE 44 *MESHOMASIC STATE FOREST*

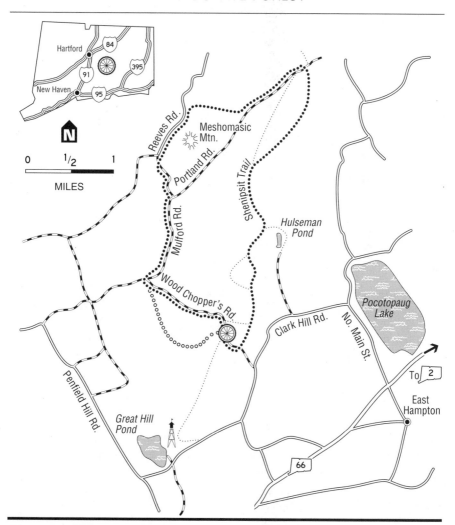

At a 4-way intersection, turn sharply left, picking up the blue-dashed trail again, and then veer to the right on it. At a T junction (just west of Hulseman Pond), turn left. Then fork right again off the blue-dashed trail, onto another single-track trail. (You can also continue on the blue-dashed trail.) This unmarked single-track trail comes out on gravel Portland Road.

Turn left on the road and, while descending, turn right sharply onto a double-track trail. (You can also continue on Portland Road.) Keep descending and veering to the right on this trail and, after a steep downhill, you will reach a small clearing. Veer left through it and you'll soon come out on an old asphalt road (Reeves Road). Turn left, descend, and watch for a hard left turn onto dirt Mulford Road. Then turn left again at the next intersection, onto Wood Chopper's Road.

For more trail riding, watch for a double-track trail turning off Wood Chopper's Road on the right soon after the junction with Mulford Road. This trail eventually forks left and comes out near the parking area. Otherwise, after about 1.5 miles on Wood Chopper's Road, you will reach the trailhead on the left.

RIDE 45 *SHENIPSIT STATE FOREST*

Woods, woods, everywhere, and lots of trails to link in this large forest (6,200 acres). It's a favorite local riding spot. This fairly challenging 12-mile loop ride explores a dozen or so single-track trails, ending at a lookout tower on Soapstone Mountain (1,061 feet) near the trailhead. About two miles of the ride also use secluded dirt roads. You will roll up and down, with only a moderate amount of climbing but plenty of loose rock and minor obstructions in places. Part of the challenge here is staying oriented on a network of trails that weave south and then north. Group rides often congregate at the trailhead on weekend mornings.

Soapstone Mountain, with its fire tower/lookout, is named after a soft rock that was quarried here until 1888. (There's a nearby foot trail to the quarry.) The stone was first mined by Native Americans, who left behind stone hatchets and arrowheads.

A piece of historical trivia: the "notch" in the otherwise straight border between Massachusetts and Connecticut was given to Massachusetts in 1804 as compensation for several towns near Shenipsit that seceded from the Colony of Massachusetts in 1734.

General location: This forest lies in Somers, off CT 190, 20 miles northeast of Hartford.

Elevation change: You will begin riding at 700′, climb to 800′, descend to 600′, and then climb to 1,000′. Finally, it's a steep descent on pavement to 700′, for a total elevation gain of about 1,000′.

Season: Any time between late spring and late fall is good for riding here. Autumn brings glowing maples and oaks throughout the forest.

Services: All services are available in Somers and south in Vernon, including the Cycle Center, (203) 872-7740, which is an active mountain bike shop with an off-road racing team and group rides.

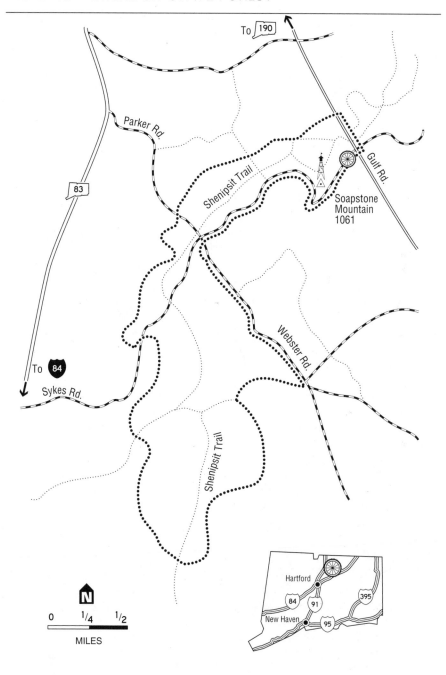

Preparing to ride. Shenipsit State Forest, Somers, Connecticut.

Hazards: There are no major hazards, but watch out for debris on some of the trails, in particular loose twigs that can jump up and snap a derailleur.

Rescue index: At most you will be about 3 miles from help on secluded trails.

Land status: State forest trails and roads.

Maps: Contact the Bureau of Parks and Forests (see below). Not all of the trails in this forest are shown on the official trail map.

Finding the trail: On Interstate 84, just east of Hartford, take Exit 63 onto CT 83 North toward South Windsor. After 13 miles, turn right onto CT 190 in Somers. After 1 mile, turn right onto Gulf Road and, after about 1 mile, you will reach a paved road on the right that leads up to the lookout on Soapstone Mountain. Park at the wide turnoffs at the bottom of this access road. From the north, take Exit 73 off I-84 onto CT 190 and head west through Stafford. After another couple of miles, turn right onto Gulf Road.

Sources of additional information:

Cycle Center
Post Road Plaza (just off I-84)
Vernon, CT 06066
(203) 872-7740

Bureau of Parks and Forests
Department of Environmental Protection
165 Capital Avenue
Hartford, CT 06106
(203) 566-2305

Notes on the trail: There are many turns on this 12-mile loop. However, the ride stays on clearly defined trails, and many are marked by blue or yellow blazes. Also, you can use wide dirt Parker Road and Webster Road to orient yourself. A topographical map and compass will also be helpful.

Ride back north on paved Gulf Road for a short distance and turn left into the woods on the *second* double-track trail along the road, just after a house. (The first trail is the Shenipsit Trail, a blue-blazed hiking trail.) Then fork left (after about a mile). After another half mile, you will come out on a double-track trail. Veer left (south), almost immediately fork right and then left again. (You can "bail out" on the double-track trail by heading straight on it, soon reaching the dirt access road to the lookout tower.)

At 2.3 miles, after a rocky downhill, veer to the right and you will reach dirt Parker Road. Turn left on the road and take the first double-track trail on the right, staying to the right at the next intersection. You will join a blue-dashed trail and continue climbing. At the next fork, turn right off the blue-dashed trail.

You will cross a second dirt road (this is about 4 miles into the ride). (For a shorter ride, turn left on the road and climb to the lookout tower.) Cross the road and continue on a single-track trail. At a T junction, turn left, heading south. You will cross a narrow dirt road. Turn left at the next fork, and then right onto a blue-dashed trail for a short distance, then fork left onto a narrower double-track trail.

Just before you reach a large logging clearing (at the southern end of the ride), turn almost 180 degrees to the left, now heading north. You will reach a T junction; turn right (toward Webster Road). When you come out on the wide unpaved Webster Road, turn left, continue until you intersect the unpaved Parker Road, turn right on it, and climb to the lookout tower. Take the paved road down from the tower toward the trailhead on Gulf Road.

RIDE 46 *SCHOOLHOUSE BROOK PARK*

Don't be misled by its tame name—this park has some stimulating riding in it. You can construct a five-mile loop on grassy and rocky single- and double-track trails through this compact, well-maintained area. Along the way, you'll pass two ponds, moss-covered boulders, delicate new growth, and, on the Juniper and Tamarack trails to the northeast, an area lined with handsome evergreen

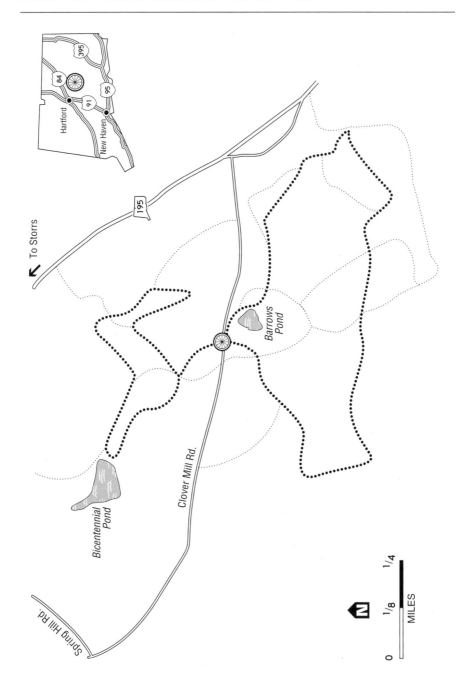

trees. Other natural attractions include Barrow's Pond (on the Barrow's Trail) and Bicentennial Pond (to the north). Hikers also use these trails.

You'll find swimming and picnicking at Bicentennial Pond, which has a sandy beach and a bathhouse. The pond is reachable from the Road Runner Trail or a paved road. (Don't ride on the trail around the pond.) For cultural and social offerings, including eateries and hangouts, there's the large University of Connecticut in nearby Storrs.

General location: The park is 3 miles south of Storrs (and "UConn," the University of Connecticut), 9 miles south of Interstate 84, and 25 miles east of Hartford.
Elevation change: This terrain is relatively flat, with some short hills. Some side trails have more challenging climbs.
Season: You can ride in this park year-round, but cyclists are asked to stay off the trails in wet weather, especially in spring. During the winter, some trails are also used by cross-country skiers. Avoid riding across their tracks.
Services: All services are available in Storrs and Willimantic, including Scott Cyclery on Main Street in Willimantic, (203) 423-6858, which is an active mountain bike shop.
Hazards: In autumn you must be watchful for minor obstructions (loose rocks and logs) that may be hidden by leaves. Also, slow down around blind corners to avoid frightening occasional hikers.
Rescue index: At most you will be about a half mile from a traveled road.
Land status: Town public trails. Local mountain bikers help maintain these trails, set guidelines, and educate bicyclists. The rules for mountain biking are posted on a board at the parking area. These include: yielding to pedestrians, walking through muddy areas, respecting water bars, not creating turnouts, and limiting group rides to five.
Maps: Trail maps are stocked in a box outside the Parks and Recreation Office inside the Town Hall in Storrs, (203) 429-3321, which is located at the junction of CT 195 and CT 275.
Finding the trail: Take Exit 68 on I-84 and head south on CT 195. After about 8 miles you will reach Storrs. Continue on CT 195 and, about 2.7 miles south of Storrs, turn right sharply onto Clover Mill Road. After a half mile, you will reach an unpaved parking lot with a park sign on the right.

Sources of additional information:

Parks and Recreation Department
Town Hall
Storrs, CT 06268
(203) 429-3321

Notes on the trail: Most of the trails are marked with names on wooden signposts ("Oak Ridge," "Bird Loop," "Pine Ridge"). On the trail map, a legend ranks the trails according to difficulty (for cross-country skiing).

A leaf-covered trail past an old stone wall. Schoolhouse Brook Park, Mansfield, Connecticut.

About two-thirds of the loops fan out to the left (southeast) of Clover Mill Road, while the others head northwest. To do a 2.5-mile loop to the southeast, ride across the paved road from the parking lot and veer right onto Stone Bridge Trail (white rectangles). After about a mile, following white blazes, you will reach blue-blazed Barrow's Trail. Turn right and continue east. After passing a field on the right, turn sharply left (still on Barrow's Trail). While climbing, turn right onto Heritage Trail (also white blazes). You will reach secluded Barrow's Pond, near Clover Mill Road.

Several scenic trails interconnect northwest of the parking area. To make a large counterclockwise loop, begin on the Road Runner Trail, turn right onto Nipmuck Trail, right onto Juniper Trail, and right again onto Tamarack Trail. Then loop to the left, heading northwest toward Bicentennial Pond, and then south on the Road Runner Trail.

RIDE 47 *MANSFIELD HOLLOW SKI TRAIL*

Here's a five-mile loop that will entertain both novice and experienced riders. Most of the ride rolls over single-track trails; the rest uses double-track trails, with a short stretch on an unpaved road. These paths circumvent a large lake. Along the way, you will pass through a variety of landscapes: piney woods, a sunny wetland of new growth, a hardwood forest, a river shoreline, and a ball field. The trails are kept in fairly good condition (for cross-country skiing), with a bit of wetness and an occasional minor obstruction. Says one local rider: "I just keep looping around—it's hard to stop."

This is a popular recreation area near the large University of Connecticut in Storrs. A canoe regatta is held on the lake each summer. You might also ride up to the massive Mansfield Hollow Dam to the south. The dams and dikes are used for flood control.

General location: The loop is in Mansfield Hollow State Park, located 4 miles south of the University of Connecticut in Storrs, 10 miles south of Interstate 84, and 26 miles due east of Hartford.

Elevation change: This overall flat terrain has many short, not-too-steep climbs and descents.

Season: Summer and fall are the best seasons for riding here. If you ride in winter, be sure not to disturb cross-country ski tracks.

Services: All services are available in Storrs and Willimantic, including an active bike shop called Scott Cyclery on Main Street in Willimantic, (203) 423-6858.

Hazards: None, except for other trail users and the occasional minor obstruction.

Rescue index: You will be about 1 mile from a traveled road.

Land status: State park trails.

Maps: Trail maps are stocked in a box outside the Parks and Recreation office inside the Town Hall in Storrs, (203) 429-3321. The Town Hall is located at the junction of CT 195 and CT 275.

Finding the trail: Take Exit 68 on I-84 and head south on CT 195. After about 8 miles, you will reach Storrs. Continue south on CT 195 for about 3.5 miles and turn left at a stoplight, passing a sign for a recreation area and Bassett Bridge Road. Then you cross a dike and pass a large field on the left. Continue until the road reaches a bridge with a large parking lot just before it on the left. Park there.

Sources of additional information:

Mansfield Hollow State Park
(202) 455-9057

RIDE 47 *MANSFIELD HOLLOW SKI TRAIL*

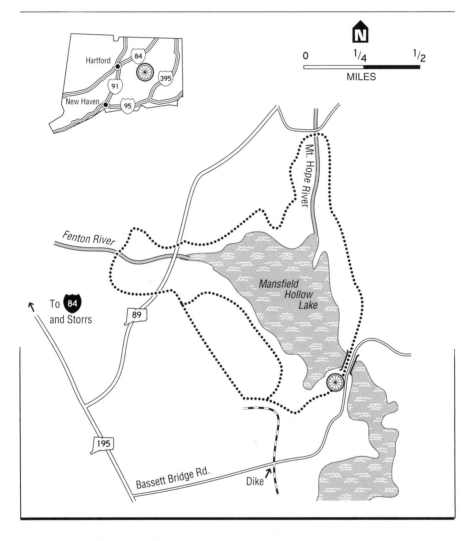

Bureau of Parks and Forests
Department of Environmental Protection
165 Capital Avenue
Hartford, CT 06106
(203) 566-2305

Parks and Recreation Department
Town Hall

Descending on semi-technical terrain. Mansfield Hollow State Park. Mansfield Hollow, Connecticut.

Storrs, CT 06268
(203) 429-3321

Notes on the trail: This cross-country ski trail is blazed with blue arrows. Begin riding clockwise around the lake, heading into the woods above the parking area. For a more challenging single-track stretch, just before reaching a wider trail on a dike, turn right into the woods onto a single-track trail and follow it around the lake until it comes out on the wider trail after a little more than a mile. Then turn right on this trail and soon reach a gate at a large ball field on paved CT 89.

Cross the field and the road and pick up the blue-arrowed trail on the other side (there's a trail sign at this trailhead).

Just keep following the blue arrows. *A tricky turn:* Just after you cross a small wooden bridge in a wetland, another blue-blazed trail forks to the left, with blue *squares* on it. Don't take it. (This left-hand trail reaches a paved road after another half mile or so, and then turns into a barely passable single-track trail.) After crossing the bridge and veering right, go uphill and keep veering toward the blue arrows. The trail winds past a landfill site, onto a dirt road, across CT 89 again, around the northern shore of the lake, across a paved bridge, and finally south toward the parking lot and boat launching area.

RIDE 48   *JAMES L. GOODWIN STATE FOREST*

This fairly challenging ride begins at a well-maintained forest conservation center, with a large pond surrounded by a lawn, handsome stone walls, and a tree farm. The ride departs from this pastoral setting for a moderately challenging ten-mile loop on five types of paths: a mile or so on a couple of secluded paved roads, about three miles on challenging single-track trails, several miles on two-wheel-drive forest roads, two miles on a rail-trail, and a mile or so on double-track trails. (For shorter rides, you can take an intersecting trail or road.)

Some stretches of the single-track trail at the beginning of the ride are strewn with rocks, requiring good bike handling skills. Also, to stay oriented in the woods, look for blue blazes on the trees. To the north, the ride joins the Natchaug State Forest ride. For easier riding, use the double-track trails around Brown Hill Pond near the trailhead.

James Goodwin, Connecticut's most famous conservationist, donated this area (2,200 acres) to the state in 1964. In 1913, he wrote: "One has only to look at the abundance of picturesque hills and valleys and streams in the state, once thickly covered with dense forests where Indians roamed, and now rapidly becoming despoiled of their freshness, to realize that there exist few more attractive and at the same time more accessible spots than we have in Connecticut."

General location: This ride lies northeast of Willimantic, off US 6.
Elevation change: There is a moderately steep half-mile climb (from Morey Road to Kingsbury Road); the rest of the ride is relatively flat, with some regular short hills.
Season: This is a 4-season ride. October and November are fall foliage months, while there is shade in the summer. In winter, avoid crossing ski-touring tracks.
Services: All services are available in Willimantic on US 6, including an active mountain bike shop, Scott Cyclery, on Main Street, (203) 423-6858.

A narrow trail in deep woods. James L. Goodwin State Forest, Hampton, Connecticut.

Hazards: Some sections of the single-track trails on the first 3 miles are covered with rocks and other minor obstructions.

Rescue index: At most you will be about 1 mile from help on secluded trails.

Land status: State forest trails and woods roads. (Blue-blazed trails, which are found throughout Connecticut, are not officially open for mountain biking. However, forest policies are established by local forest rangers.)

Maps: A trail map may be available at the forest headquarters. Or you can contact the Bureau of Parks and Forests (see below).

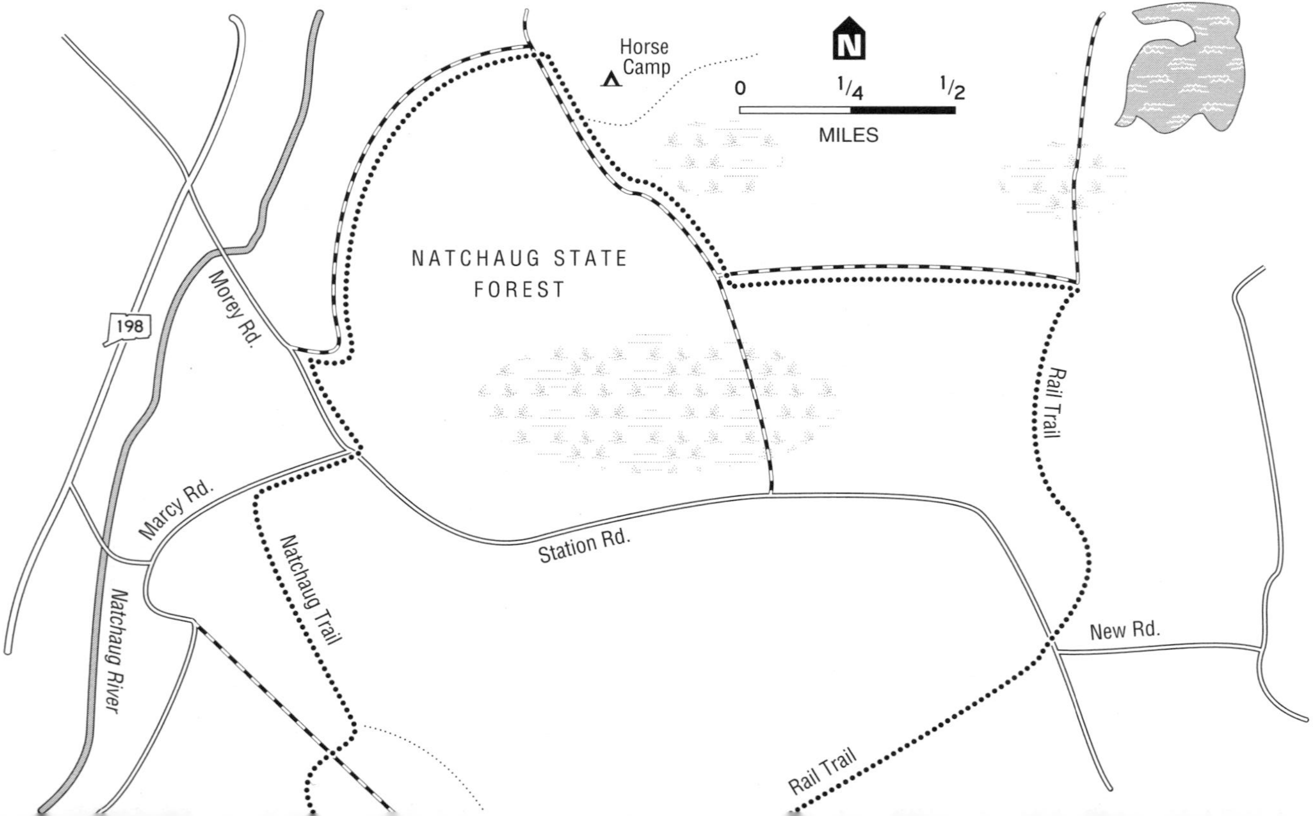

RIDE 48 *JAMES L. GOODWIN STATE FOREST*

Rail Trail

New Rd.

Rail Trail

Horse
Camp

N

1/4   1/2

0

MILES

NATCHAUG STATE
FOREST

Station Rd.

Natchaug Trail

Morey Rd.

Marcy Rd.

198

Natchaug River

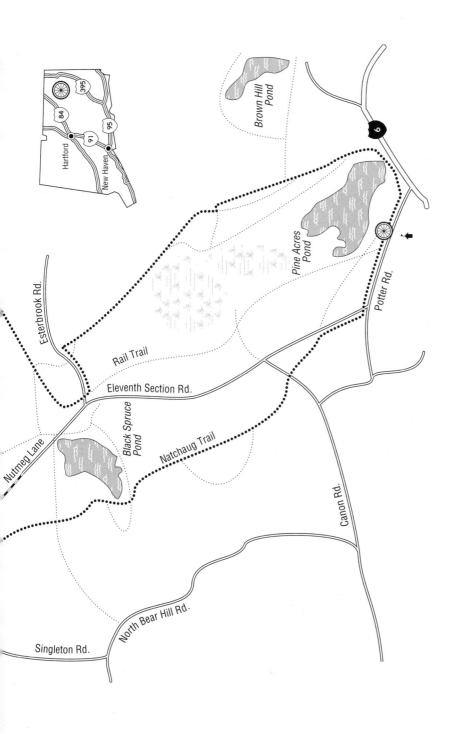

Brown Hill Pond

Pine Acres Pond

Esterbrook Rd.

Rail Trail

Eleventh Section Rd.

Black Spruce Pond

Natchaug Trail

Nutmeg Lane

Potter Rd.

Canon Rd.

North Bear Hill Rd.

Singleton Rd.

395

84

91

95

Hartford

New Haven

6

Finding the trail: On US 6, follow the brown state forest signs. The access road, Potter Road, is 1.2 miles west of the junction of CT 97 and US 6. Drive up the access road to a parking area on the right, just across from the headquarters building.

Sources of additional information:

James L. Goodwin State Forest
Hampton, CT 06247
(203) 455-9534
Rangers are posted at the Conservation Center across from the parking lot. Drop in for a chat.

Bureau of Parks and Forests
Department of Environmental Protection
165 Capital Avenue
Hartford, CT 06106
(203) 566-2305

Notes on the trail: At the beginning and end of this ride you will be on a network of single-track trails with many junctions. Things can seem confusing at times. Remember, however, that the area is compact. You also can stay oriented by never heading too far east or west.

To begin, ride up paved Potter Road for almost a half mile and turn right onto paved Eleventh Section Road. After a short distance, watch for a break in a stone wall on the left with a trail heading uphill. Turn left on this trail; you'll soon reach the dirt Canon Road. Make a dogleg turn to the left and right, picking up the trail on the other side. This trail will blend into a double-track trail, still heading north.

After a short distance, you can turn left onto a single-track trail for a short, technical side trail that loops back to this trail. Otherwise, continue and turn left at a fork, pass through a 4-way intersection (Black Spruce Pond is on the right through the woods), veer right onto a woods road, go through another 4-way intersection, and come out at a wooden gate at unpaved Nutmeg Lane. Dogleg to the left and right, and pick up another gated woods road. You will reach a clearing and turn left, toward a blue arrow, passing through an opening in a stone wall. Follow the blue blazes on this single-track.

You will come out at paved Marcy Road. Turn right on the pavement, and left at the next intersection onto paved Morey Road. (To shorten the ride, turn right onto Morey Road, which becomes Station Road, and pick up the rail-trail on the right after about 2 miles.) While descending on Morey Road, turn sharply right onto an unpaved woods road. You will climb and reach a T junction with Kingsbury Road in Natchaug State Forest.

Turn right, then left at the first major fork and, when this wide woods road veers sharply left, fork right onto a double-track rail-trail. (The Natchaug State Forest ride, Ride 49, turns left.) On the rail-trail you will cross Station Road, and reach paved Esterbrook Road. Turn left on the pavement and watch for a white-blazed single-track trail on the right. Turn right on it and, at a T junction with a woods road, turn right again, and then fork left onto another single-track trail. At the next trail junction, turn left onto a red-blazed trail. Continue south, or turn left for a side loop around Brown Hill Pond.

RIDE 49 *NATCHAUG STATE FOREST*

Crank along these 6.5 miles of secluded woods roads at a fast pace, or cruise and take in the scenery: hardwood trees that turn bright orange and red in autumn, giant evergreens, marshland, a river, and a lake. Two-wheel-drive dirt and gravel roads make up most of this moderately easy loop ride, with an optional 1.5-mile "shortcut" on a more rugged double-track trail, and about a mile on old asphalt. You might stop on the last stretch at a scenic picnic and recreational area along the Natchaug River, relaxing under groves of hemlocks.

The marshland on the eastern edge of this large forest (12,500 acres) is a favorite bird-watching area, as well as a place for watching other wildlife—if you're quiet. On the northern edge of the ride, you will pass by a quail farm. This ride can be linked with the James L. Goodwin State Forest ride, which joins it to the south.

General location: The forest is just off CT 198, between US 44 and US 6.
Elevation change: In a counterclockwise direction, you will begin by climbing gently and steadily for about a mile, then rolling for about 4 miles, and finally climbing fairly steeply on pavement for the last 1.5 miles.
Season: This is a 4-season ride. It's well drained in the spring, shady in the summer, colorful in the fall, and quiet in the winter.
Services: All services are available in Willimantic, including Scott Cyclery on Main Street, (203) 423-6858, which is an active mountain bike shop. There's camping at several campgrounds along CT 198.
Hazards: None, except for occasional horseback riders (yield to them), occasional hikers on the trails, and motorized vehicles on the roads.
Rescue index: At most you will be about 2 miles from help.
Land status: State forest roads and trails.
Maps: Maps are available from the Bureau of Parks and Forests (see below).
Finding the trail: From US 44, turn south onto CT 198. You will reach the forest entrance on the left after about 3 miles. From US 6, turn north on CT 198, and then right at a small brown sign for the state forest. Climb an asphalt access road until you reach a T junction after seven-tenths of a mile. Turn right onto a dirt road, and almost immediately left onto another dirt road, toward the Beaver Dam Wildlife Management Area. You will reach a parking area almost immediately.

RIDE 49 *NATCHAUG STATE FOREST*

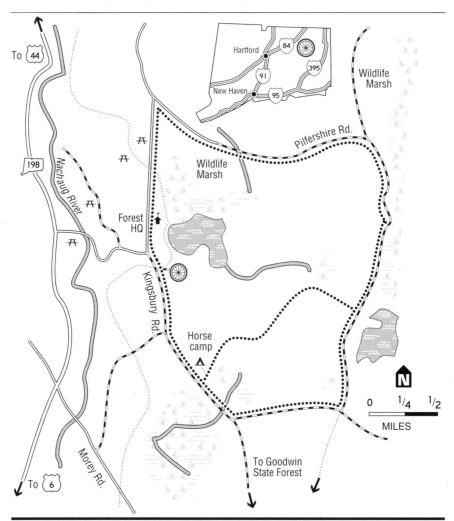

Sources of additional information:

Bureau of Parks and Forests
Department of Environmental Protection
165 Capital Avenue
Hartford, CT 06106
(203) 566-2305

Cruising through a state forest. Natchaug State Forest, Eastford, Connecticut.

Notes on the trail: This ride is easy to follow. Turn left at all major intersections (with an optional left-hand shortcut on a trail). Ride south on unpaved Kingsbury Road, fork left, and fork left again, passing a reservoir on the right. To do some trail riding, turn left onto a narrow dirt road just under 1 mile from the beginning of the ride. You'll soon reach a fork. To the left is the Silvermine Horse Camp area; to the right a trail enters the woods, rejoining the other side of the loop.

Or you can continue on Kingsbury Road, making 2 sharp left turns, and you'll be heading north. (Turning *right* at any one of the preceding forks will take you toward the James L. Goodwin State Forest; see Ride 48.) Fork left again, onto dirt Pilfershire Road, which crosses a brook, becomes paved, and climbs. When it levels off, turn left sharply on another paved road. You will pass a large picnic area along the river on the right and several forest headquarters buildings. Ride through the junction where you came into the forest, and then turn left to reach the parking area.

RIDE 50   *KILLINGLY POND*

This fairly challenging five-mile loop ride explores several long single-track trails, which are connected by a narrow jeep road that can be an easier out-and-back ride. Otherwise, you head off from the large Killingly Pond for rugged trails that run north-south in secluded woods. Along the way, you maneuver around some wet areas and tackle stretches of eroded terrain. At its northern end, the ride comes out near a clearing where more trails head north into the Durfee Hill Management Area in Rhode Island. (This ride is a few miles south of the George Washington Management Area ride [Ride 57] in Rhode Island.) Killingly Pond itself is a popular local swimming spot.

General location: Just east of Exit 93 on Interstate 395; half of this ride is in Rhode Island.

Elevation change: This is rolling terrain, with one moderately steep climb of about 200' on a rugged trail.

Season: Any time between May and October is good for riding here.

Services: All services are available along CT 101 and in Danielson, where there is a full-service mountain bike shop, Ordinary Bike Shop, (203) 774-1660.

Hazards: Watch for occasional minor obstructions on the trail, especially when descending. Also, these trails are unmarked, so it is possible to get disoriented. If you do, head south and you will cross the unpaved Snake Hill Road.

Rescue index: You will be about 1 mile at most from help.

Land status: Public trails on public and private land.

Maps: The map in this book is the best map of these trails available.

Finding the trail: Take Exit 93 on I-395 and head east on CT 101. After about 4.5 miles, you will reach the Rhode Island border. Park at a turnoff area on the right just before the border. There is a turnoff for only a few cars at Killingly Pond; that parking spot is usually filled in summer. After parking on CT 101, ride down Riley Chase Road until you reach paved Pond Road. Fork right and you will reach the pond on the right.

Sources of additional information: Ordinary Bike Shop, Main Street, Danielson, (203) 774-1660. This is an active mountain bike shop, with weekly group rides.

Notes on the trail: Although this isn't a complex network of trails, it can be somewhat hard to follow at times because they're unmarked. Also, the trail becomes faint in 1 or 2 places, but it is never overgrown. Be prepared to stop or slow down once in a while to check out the trail and get your bearings. Also, a few stretches of trail are heavily eroded or possibly obstructed with fallen trees. But the trails are passable—and the payoff is worth it.

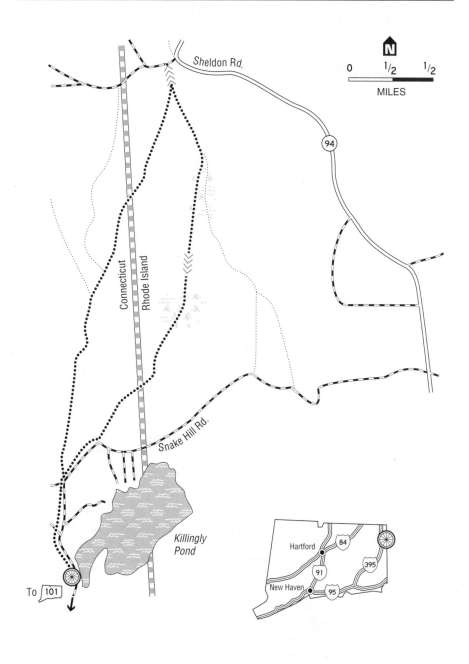

Sheldon Rd.

N

0   1/2   1/2

MILES

94

Connecticut

Rhode Island

Snake Hill Rd.

Killingly
Pond

To 101

Hartford   84

91   395

New Haven   95

Coasting downhill. Killingly Pond, East Killingly, Connecticut.

Ride up Pond Road past the pond for a few hundred yards and turn right onto a jeep road into the woods. After about a half mile, you will come out at a T junction with a wider dirt road, Snake Hill Road. Just across from this junction is the return trail for this ride. Turn right onto Snake Hill Road, and then take the next left fork, after about a half mile, onto a double-track trail. (Snake Hill Road goes to the right.) *A tricky turn:* Just after riding through a low-lying, marshy area for a few feet, while climbing, fork left onto the trail that lies just behind a large fallen tree. You will then go through a wet, eroded section (known as "the ditch"), before the trail becomes smoother and drier.

Next, while descending, you intersect a trail coming in from the right, and then another one on the left. At the second trail, you can turn sharply left to complete this loop, or else keep descending northward for a short distance, coming out on a dirt road. Turn right and you will reach paved RI 94, at a small clearing next to a stream. More trails head north out of this field.

Then return up the trail you came down, and take the first fork right. To avoid a couple of muddy sections on this trail, fork right onto "jug handle" trails that reconnect with the main trail. After a fun descent you reach Snake Hill Road. Take the trail on the other side to return to the pond, or turn left on the road and pick up another trail off it heading north.

RIDE 51 *PACHAUG STATE FOREST*

This largest forest in Connecticut (24,000 acres) boasts some of the most scenic and convenient woods-road riding in southern New England, as well as about 20 miles of technical single-track trails. It's well worth a trip to this less-settled part of the state to explore these secluded, sunny roads and winding trails. You can also relax at one of the many picnic sites, do a short hike to a lookout on Mt. Misery, or stretch out at secluded Phillips Pond or busier Beachdale Pond.

This moderate nine-mile loop explores the central part of the forest, using a network of narrow two-wheel-drive roads and a double-track trail, with three optional stretches on single-track trails. Because many of the single-track trails in this forest are unmapped, however, it is best to hook up with local riders to do an all-trail ride. There are many more trails just north of this ride, and in a section of the forest east of CT 49.

General location: In the southeastern corner of Connecticut, just off Interstate 395, about 10 miles east of Norwich.
Elevation change: The roads and trails in the forest are rolling or flat, with an occasional moderate climb.
Season: If there is little snow, this is a 4-season ride. Avoid riding on the trails in wet weather.
Services: Water and restrooms are available at the trailhead and at Phillips Pond. There are first-come, first-serve campsites at Mt. Misery. All other services are available along CT 138 and in Norwich. There's a full-service mountain bike shop, Ordinary Bike Shop, in Danielson, (203) 774-1660.
Hazards: Watch for occasional motorized traffic on the dirt roads, especially on summer weekends. Yield to hikers and horseback riders. If you decide to explore the single-track trails on your own, be aware that many of them are blazed with identical blue markings. In other words, being on a blue-blazed trail doesn't necessarily mean you're on the same trail on which you began riding.

RIDE 51 *PACHAUG STATE FOREST*

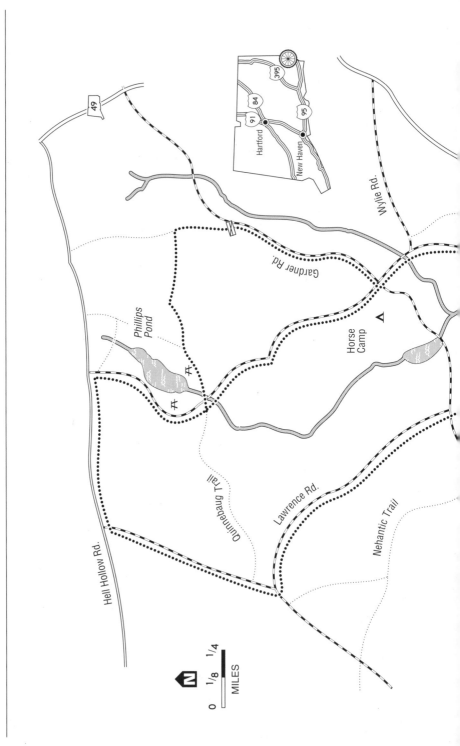

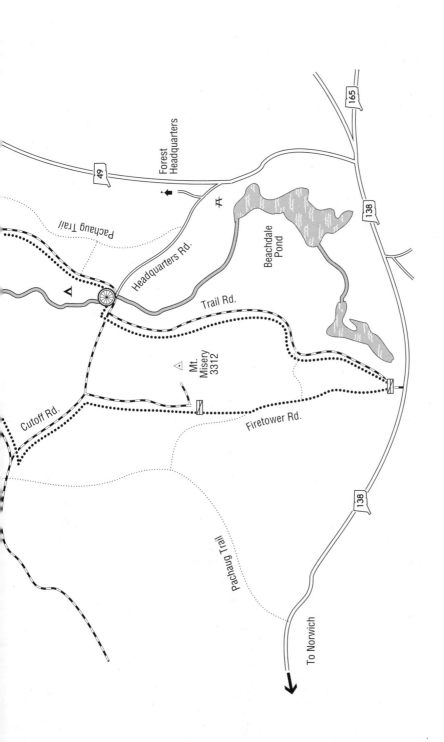

49

Forest
Headquarters

Pachaug Trail

Headquarters Rd.

Beachdale
Pond

Trail Rd.

△ Mt.
Misery
3312

Cutoff Rd.

Firetower Rd.

Pachaug Trail

165

138

138

To Norwich

Rescue index: At most you will be about 1 mile from help.

Land status: Roads and trails in a public forest.

Maps: The Bureau of Parks and Forests (see "Sources of additional information") offers a fairly good map of the dirt roads and of several major trails. However, many of the single-track trails in this forest are unmapped.

Finding the trail: From I-395, take Exit 85 and head east on CT 138. After several miles, turn left (north) onto CT 49. You can also reach CT 49 by heading east on CT 165. After about a half mile on CT 49, you will see a small brown state forest sign on the left at the forest access road. Turn left onto this paved road. You can park at a lot near CT 49, or drive up the access road for seven-tenths of a mile to a large lot on the left.

Sources of additional information:

Bureau of Parks and Forests
Department of Environmental Protection
165 Capital Avenue
Hartford, CT 06106
(203) 566-2305

Notes on the trail: If you stay on the dirt roads, this 9-mile loop is easy to follow. You can take shorter rides by turning back toward the parking area at several junctions. Begin by heading north from the camping area on Trail Road. Continue through 2 intersections, past Phillips Pond, and you will come out on paved Hell Hollow Road. Turn left and pick up the next dirt road to the left. At the next intersection, turn left onto dirt Lawrence Road, right at the next intersection, and then left onto Cutoff Road.

Now you can continue back to the trailhead, or turn right onto Firetower Road, which passes the trailhead for Mt. Misery and then becomes a gated double-track trail. When this trail reaches a gate at the southern edge of the forest, turn sharply left onto Trail Road, which heads back to the parking area.

Three single-track options: Begin on the blue-blazed Pachaug Trail, which forks off the paved access road a short distance from CT 49. The trail comes out on Wylie Road. Turn left and right onto Trail Road. (The Pachaug Trail north of Wylie Road is not passable.)

At the next 4-way intersection, turn right onto Gardner Road and, after about a mile, you will pass a gated double-track trail on the left. Turn onto it, and at the next intersection turn left onto another double-track trail, and then right at the next intersection. You will come out at Phillips Pond. (*Note:* There are more interconnecting trails in this area.)

Just west of Phillips Pond, you can pick up the Quinnebaug Trail, which winds west, coming out on a dirt road near Lawrence Road. More trails wind south from here toward Firetower Road.

A woods road with trailheads. Pachaug State Forest, Pachaug, Connecticut.

RHODE ISLAND

RIDE 52 *GREAT SWAMP MANAGEMENT AREA*

This easy six-mile loop ride circumvents a scenic wetland on several narrow, grassy roads that turn into double-track trails. You can crank along at a fast pace, but then you'll miss the scenery and wildlife. About a third of the ride skirts a large wetland, where you might spy waterfowl nesting. In autumn, the maples and other deciduous trees bordering this "swamp" show off their colors. There's also an out-and-back side trail to the grassy shore of large Worden Pond, and an inner loop that climbs to a modest view.

If you're visiting Rhode Island, you might take in Newport (on RI 138 to the east) with its public beaches, historic mansions, seafood restaurants, and world-famous folk and jazz festivals.

General location: This area is at the junction of RI 2 and RI 138, 5 miles west of Kingston.

Elevation change: The ride is relatively flat, with one short climb.

Season: Spring and fall are the best seasons for riding here, with good drainage in the spring and colorful foliage in autumn. Late fall is hunting season (see "Hazards").

Services: All services are available to the east in Kingston. Two bike shops are Stedmans, on Main Street in Wakefield, (401) 789-8664, and Kings Cycle, on Post Road in Westerly, (401) 322-6005.

Hazards: Great Swamp is a popular hunting site from mid-October through December. The rangers suggest that mountain bicyclists not use the management area during this time. Check at the headquarters on the access road for hunting dates each year.

Rescue index: You will be about 1 mile from help on easily traversed terrain.

Land status: Roads in a public management area.

Maps: A map and other information are available at the headquarters on the access road.

Finding the trail: Take Exit 3A on Interstate 95, onto RI 138 toward Kingston and Newport. From Providence take RI 2 to RI 138 and turn left. After about 8 miles, cross RI 2 and continue until you pass a sign on the right for the Great Swamp Management Area, just before the junction with RI 110. Turn right and follow this road until it becomes unpaved, passes a cluster of fish and wildlife headquarters buildings on the right, enters the secluded management area, and reaches an unpaved parking area.

RIDE 52 *GREAT SWAMP MANAGEMENT AREA*

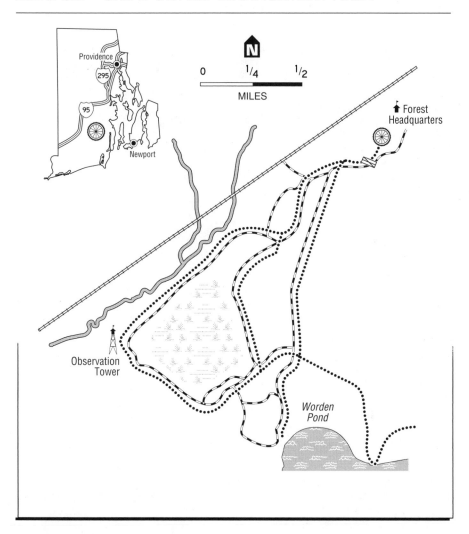

Sources of additional information:

Division of Fish and Wildlife
Wakefield, RI 02879
(401) 789-3094 or (401) 277-3075

Notes on the trail: This loop ride is easy to follow. To take the large loop, fork right just under a half mile, then right again at one mile. Follow the trail as it

Circumventing a wetland. Great Swamp Management Area, Kingston, Rhode Island.

winds around the wetland. After passing the shoreline of the "swamp," you will reach another fork. Take the left fork for a shorter, elevated trail back to the trailhead. Otherwise, fork right. You will reach a 3-way intersection. Turn right for a half-mile side trip to Worden Pond. Otherwise, fork left and head back to the parking area. Then loop around again, exploring the paths you skipped the first time.

RIDE 53 *ARCADIA MANAGEMENT AREA*

This most popular mountain biking site in Rhode Island draws riders from as far away as Boston and Hartford. They come to tackle 30 miles or so of secluded single-track trails. For those seeking less technical riding, several miles of scenic dirt roads crisscross in this 10,000-acre forest.

This fairly challenging 12-mile ride follows a perimeter loop on mainly single-track trails, winding through a highly diverse landscape of large pine trees, smaller hardwoods, mountain laurel and other bushes, ferns and grasses, a large pond, and streams. You might also see wildlife, including deer. In the center of the management area is Breakheart Pond, a pleasant place to take a break. Finally, four miles east of Arcadia on RI 165 is a sandy beach at a huge pond that straddles the Rhode Island-Connecticut border.

General location: The management area is located just a few miles from Interstate 95, and 25 miles southwest of Providence.

Elevation change: Although the area is relatively flat, many single-track trails roll up and down. The dirt roads are flatter.

Season: This is a 4-season ride. Expect some mud, though, in the spring and any time after a rainfall.

Services: Be sure to bring plenty of water, for there is no water available in the management area. All services are available along RI 102 and RI 3, and in Hope Valley to the south.

Hazards: Watch for horseback riders and hikers (a local hiking club meets here). If you ride during the hunting season, usually from late November through December, wear bright clothing. Check with the area manager for hunting dates (see below).

Rescue index: At most you will be about 2 miles from help on secluded trails.

Land status: Old roads and trails on public land.

Maps: The Department of Environmental Management has a rough trail map. A better one is produced by the Rhode Island Fat Tire Club (see below).

Finding the trail: Take Exit 5A on I-95, onto RI 102 South. Veer right onto RI 3 South (following signs for RI 165). Turn right at a blinking light onto RI 165 West. After about 2.5 miles, you will reach a small white church on the right. You can park in front of the church, or turn right after the church and park in a parking area. Lock your vehicle.

Sources of additional information:

Rhode Island Fat Tire Club
245 Old Coach Road
Charlestown, RI 02877
(401) 364-0786

Department of Environmental Management
Arcadia Management Area
(401) 539-2356

Notes on the trail: You can easily take at least 2 completely different rides here: an intricate loop on single-track trails, or a less technical and simpler ride on dirt roads. The 12-mile ride described here uses quite a few trails. Almost the entire ride, however, is blazed with yellow dots (and white and orange dots on 2 trails at the end of the ride). To paraphrase a famous movie line: *Follow the yellow-dot trail.*

Here's a turn-by-turn description of this counterclockwise loop. Ride east on

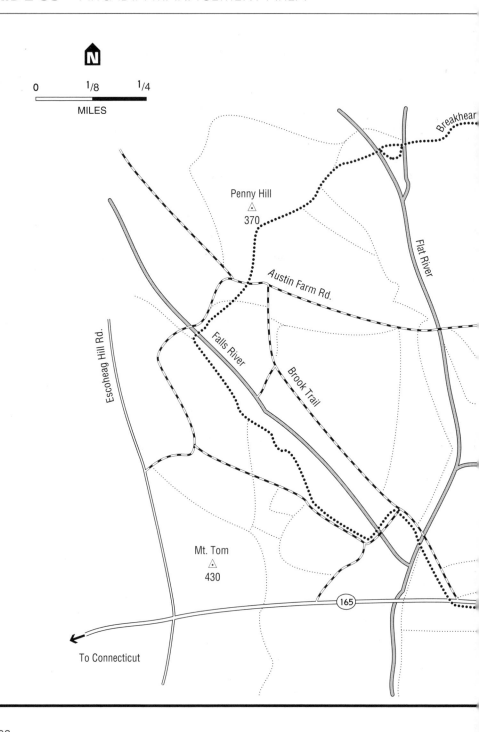

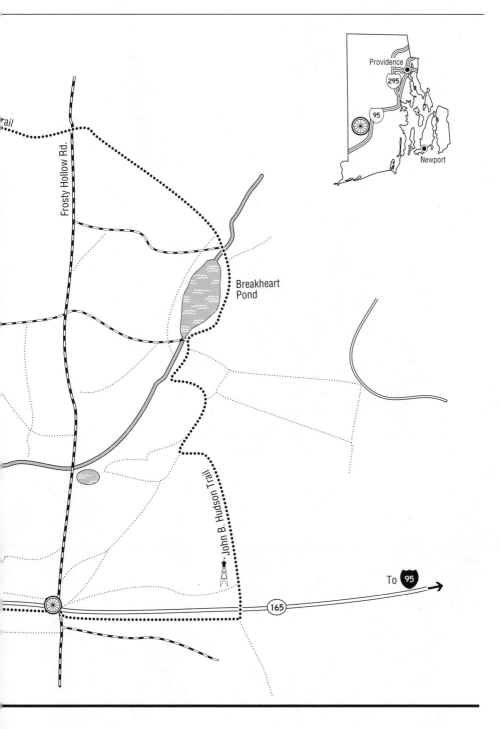

Breakheart
Pond

Frosty Hollow Rd.

John B. Hudson Trail

ail

Providence

295

95

Newport

To 95

165

Serious single-tracking. Arcadia Management Area, Hope Valley, Rhode Island.

RI 165 for about three-tenths of a mile, and turn left into the management area on a four-wheel-drive road, soon passing a board with a sign that reads, "John B. Hudson Trail, 1.6 miles." A large map of the area is located here, and a box that may contain trail maps. (A few hundred feet farther on this trail, you can take a short side trail on the left to a small observation tower.)

When you reach a narrow dirt road, turn right on it, then almost immediately fork left onto the John B. Hudson Trail at a double yellow blazing. At a small clearing, this single-track trail blends into a wider trail. Continue in the same direction (north), and you will reach Breakheart Pond.

Turn right on the dirt road in front of the pond, pass through a gate, and almost immediately turn left at the yellow blazes. After a few hundred feet, fork left where a sign tells distances and directions to several destinations. Soon you will cross a bridge. Keep right at a fork; both trail options link up later, but go right now. You will come out on a wider trail and veer right (again following the yellow blazes). When you reach a T junction with a wider trail, turn left and cross a small wooden bridge. When you pass several large boulders on the right, turn right at a white arrow and a sign for the Breakheart Trail, which is what you want.

Go through a 4-way intersection of trails, cross a dirt road, and make a dogleg turn to the right and left to pick up the yellow-blazed Breakheart Trail again. Go straight at the next intersection (following the yellow blazes). Then turn right at an intersection with a wider trail, cross a bridge, and fork left after it. Turn left at the next fork.

You will reach Penny Hill, which offers a modest view through pine trees. Continue riding southwest, cross the dirt Austin Farm Road, veer right onto another narrow dirt road, and almost immediately turn left at the yellow blazes. You come out onto a two-wheel-drive road. Turn left and cross a bridge. Almost immediately fork left onto a *white-blazed* trail, the Escoheag Trail. At the next fork, turn left onto the Sand Hill Trail, which is marked with *orange blazes*. This trail comes out on a dirt road. Turn left, pass through a gate, reach a T junction, turn left again, and cross a wooden bridge. At the next T junction, turn right and cruise down to RI 165. Turn left to return to the parking lot.

If that's not enough riding, more trails (many of them challenging) head south of RI 165.

RIDE 54   *NEW LONDON TURNPIKE*

This secluded unpaved road, which was once a major thoroughfare across Rhode Island, makes an easy out-and-back ride. The nine-mile route alternates between smooth, rolling two-wheel-drive stretches that pass fields and farms, stone walls, ponds, and occasional homes, and four-wheel-drive sections that will keep you focused on loose gravel, embedded rock, and dips. This "no-brainer" ride also bisects a state-managed area containing a network of single-track trails (see the Big River Management Area ride, Ride 55).

General location: The road parallels Interstate 95, between Exits 4 and 7, from West Warwick to Hope Valley.
Elevation change: The road is relatively flat, with gradual climbs and descents.
Season: This is a 4-season ride, with some mud in the spring.
Services: All services are available along RI 3, including Valley Mountain Bikes in West Warwick, (401) 392-3066.
Hazards: None, except for occasional traffic on the crossroads.
Rescue index: At most you will be about a half mile from help.

RIDE 54 *NEW LONDON TURNPIKE*

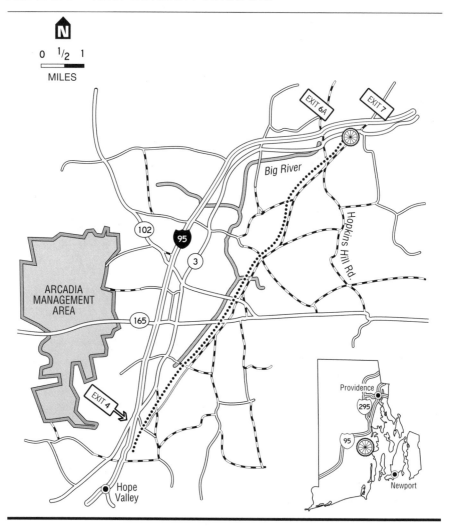

Land status: A public road.

Maps: Any detailed state road map will show the road. The state offers an excellent free state map (see below).

Finding the trail: On I-95, take Exit 7 (Coventry/West Warwick). Turn right immediately and you will reach a large commuter parking area on the right. You can park here. Continue riding up the road for a short distance and you will reach a gated dirt road. This is the northern terminus of the New London Turnpike. You can also park at turnoffs near Exit 6A or Exit 4 on I-95.

Sources of additional information:

> Department of Economic Development
> Rhode Island Tourism Bureau
> (401) 277-2601 (Rhode Island only)
> (800) 556-2484

> Valley Mountain Bikes
> Nooseneck Hill Road (Route 3)
> West Greenwich, RI 02817
> (401) 392-3066

Notes on the trail: After riding south for about 7 miles, you will reach an intersection with a small falls on the right. New London Turnpike becomes a paved road here. To extend the ride, continue south for another 2.5 miles; the first 1.5 miles is mostly paved, but the last mile is a rugged double-track trail that descends almost to I-95.

For those who don't mind riding on pavement, you can also loop back on scenic paved roads to the east, including Henry Brown Road and Hopkins Hill Road. For more technical riding, explore some of the single-track trails that cross the turnpike near its northern end (see the Big River Management Area ride).

RIDE 55 *BIG RIVER MANAGEMENT AREA*

This challenging ten-mile ride weaves through a secluded woods on some of the best single-track in southern New England. Many of these rolling, twisting trails were made years ago by motorized dirt bikes. Today, local mountain bike racers use them for honing their skills.

The ride begins and ends on a half-mile stretch of old asphalt and a short stretch on a dirt road. About a mile of the ride also uses double-track trails. The rest of the time, you're on narrow single-track trails, with plenty of roots and rocks, occasional obstructions, and a mudhole or two.

Although the trails are in good condition, some inclines are eroded, with lots of loose rock and dirt.

You can take shorter loops, as well as do less technical riding, on the jeep roads that intersect this pine and shrub forest (see the New London Turnpike ride, Ride 54). It's a pleasant, quiet setting, with pine needles carpeting some of the trails. There's more single-track riding to the east of unpaved New London Turnpike and Hopkins Hill Road.

General location: The ride is just off Exit 6 on Interstate 95, 20 miles south of Providence.

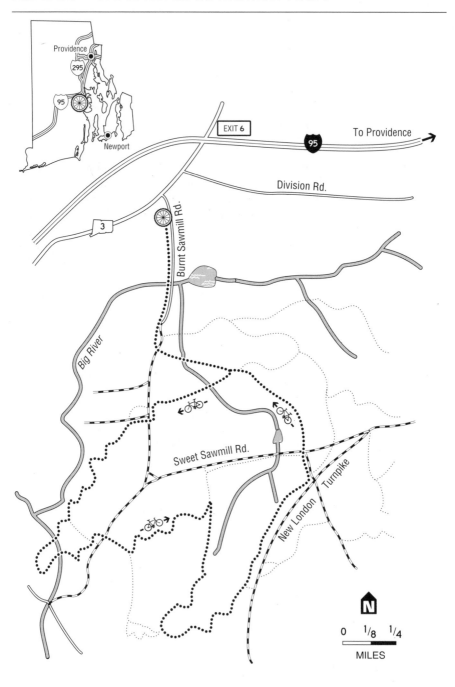

Single file on single-track. Big River Management Area, Greenwich,
Rhode Island.

Elevation change: Although the area is relatively flat, the trails roll up and down
like a roller coaster.

Season: Any time between late spring and late fall is best for riding here. Local
cyclists do ride here year-round, although late fall to early winter is hunting season. Check with the Department of Environmental Management about specific
hunting times (see below).

Services: All services are available on RI 3 and in Coventry. Valley Mountain Bikes, (401) 392-3066, is located near the trailhead on RI 3 (Nooseneck Hill
Road).

Hazards: These tight single-track trails must be ridden with concentration—

even by accomplished riders. Around any corner, a steep, eroded downhill section may await, demanding good bike handling and braking skills. Also, because this is a secluded area, you might consider carrying a detailed map and a compass.

Rescue index: At most you will be a couple of miles from help on secluded trails. As always, if you're riding in an area for the first time, it's a good idea to tell someone where you're riding and when you expect to return.

Land status: Trails and old roads through public land, managed by the state Department of Environmental Management (see below). These trails are multi-use; riders should be considerate of other trail users.

Maps: The best map of this area is produced by the Rhode Island Fat Tire Club (see below). The club is planning to blaze these trails sometime in the future. A detailed state road map will show the unpaved and paved roads that intersect and border the area.

Finding the trail: Take Exit 6 on I-95, onto RI 3. From the north, turn left onto RI 3. Within a hundred yards a small paved parking area comes up on the left, next to the trailhead and Burnt Sawmill Road. From the south, turn right onto RI 3 and reach the parking area on the left.

Sources of additional information:

Department of Environmental Management
Arcadia Management Area
(401) 539-2356

Rhode Island Fat Tire Club
245 Old Coach Road
Charlestown, RI 02822
(401) 364-0786

Notes on the trail: This is a fairly complex ride, with many turns. The entire ride uses obvious trails, however. If you find yourself on an *overgrown* trail, double back and pick up the well-ridden one. The ride also crosses a couple of dirt roads, which will help you stay oriented. The ride can be divided into 4 loops that keep extending the ride.

Loop 1: Begin by riding up old asphalt Burnt Sawmill Road, which turns to dirt after a half mile. Almost immediately after it becomes unpaved, turn left onto a double-track trail at a telephone pole. Stay on this main double-track trail and you will soon reach a T junction at a wider double-track trail. Turn right and you will reach another T junction. Turn left (this is Burnt Sawmill Road). If you look to the right, you should be able to see a gate across the road. (For a short ride, you can turn right to return to the trailhead.)

Loop 2: After turning left onto Burnt Sawmill Road, climb for a short distance and fork right onto a narrow dirt road. After about a hundred feet, turn left onto a single-track trail. Stay on this trail, bearing right, and then forking right. (For a shorter loop fork left; you will come out on the same dirt road you reach later.) Fork left at the next intersection, bear left again, and you will emerge at a 4-way intersection.

Go straight across this intersection, onto a single-track trail. You will reach another 4-way intersection. This is Sweet Sawmill Road. Go straight across it onto a narrow dirt road. (Again, for a shorter ride, turn left on the dirt road.)

Loop 3: After a short distance, fork left onto a single-track trail and you will come to a T junction. (For a shorter ride, turn left and at the next intersection go right onto a dirt road.) Otherwise, turn right, and fork right off the main trail as you're descending. Then fork left, and left again onto a single-track trail.

Continue on this trail for over a mile, crossing several mudholes. Stay on the main trail, veering to the left. You will reach another 4-way intersection. Turn left, and you will come out at another T junction on a narrow dirt road, Sweet Sawmill Road. Turn left on the road, and take an immediate right turn.

Loop 4: Continue on this narrow trail, turning left at another T junction. Take the next right turn and climb gently. You are now on the single-track trail that you came in on. Follow it until you rejoin the double-track trail. Then turn left onto Burnt Sawmill Road, and right to return to the parking area.

RIDE 56 *TRESTLE TRAIL LOOP*

This easy-to-moderate seven-mile loop ride uses scenic two-wheel-drive dirt roads (with some eroded areas), a couple of pavement stretches, and a 2.5-mile section of a rail-trail. It's classic New England countryside—you could be in Vermont or Maine. The landscape alternates between inhabited and uninhabited areas. There are stands of pine trees and wetlands, small farms, open fields, and stone walls.

The rail-trail provides a closer view of nature: light woods, new growth, and four small streams that pass beneath the trail. This flat, straight cinder path, named the Trestle Trail, extends for several miles farther to the east and west. More dirt roads extend south of this ride.

General location: The ride is at the junction of RI 102 and RI 117, 12 miles west of Warwick.
Elevation change: In a counterclockwise direction, you will begin with a steady, fairly gradual climb of about 200′, roll gently for several miles, descend for 2 miles, and end on a flat rail-trail for a couple of miles.
Season: Any time between late spring and late fall is good for riding here.
Services: At the trailhead there's a classic general store, complete with a deli. All

RIDE 56 *TRESTLE TRAIL LOOP*

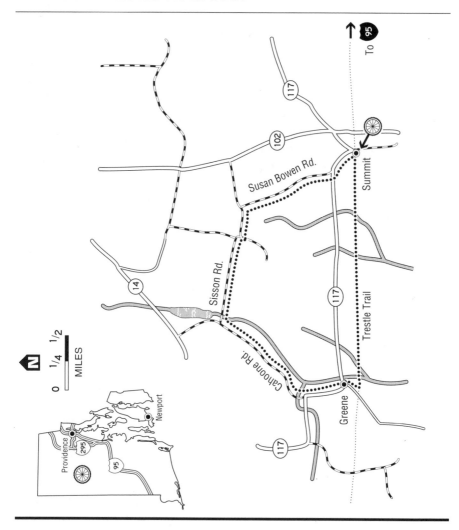

other services are available to the east on RI 117 and in West Warwick, including The Bicycle Shop on RI 117 in Coventry, (401) 822-2080.

Hazards: Be sure to yield to the occasional horse and buggy on the dirt roads; a horse farm operates nearby. Also, watch out for the occasional motorized vehicle on these narrow roads.

Rescue index: You are never far from help.

Land status: Public roads and a public trail.

Close encounter of a nineteenth-century kind. Coventry, Rhode Island.

Maps: Any detailed state road map will do. The state offers an excellent state map (see below).

Finding the trail: Take Exit 10 off Interstate 95, onto RI 117 West. After 12 miles you will reach a junction with RI 102. Continue for a short distance on RI 117 and turn left onto Old Summit Road. Almost immediately, you will reach an unpaved parking area across from a general store. The rail-trail is just beyond the store.

You can also begin with an out-and-back ride on the rail-trail at its eastern-most end. Eight miles west of I-95, on RI 117, turn left onto Hill Farm Road and almost immediately pull off the road next to the rail-trail. (*Note:* About 1.5 miles west of this trailhead, a bridge may be down, requiring a short portage across a shallow stream.)

Sources of additional information:

Department of Economic Development
Rhode Island Tourism Bureau
(401) 277-2601 (Rhode Island only); (800) 556-2484

Notes on the trail: You can begin this loop either by riding on the rail-trail or the dirt roads. The description here begins by climbing for a short distance on pavement, descends on dirt and gravel roads, and finishes on the rail-trail.

Cross RI 117 and ride up Susan Bowen Road. You will reach a T junction after about a mile. Turn left, then right, and then fork left almost immediately onto Sisson Road. You will reach a T junction with Cahoone Road after about a mile. Turn left and, after about 2 miles, Cahoone Road comes out on paved RI 117. Turn left on the pavement; after a half mile you will reach an intersection. Turn right on another paved road (RI 117 forks left).

After a short distance, you will pass a large white Masonic Lodge on the left and the rail-trail behind it. For an out-and-back side trip, turn right on the rail-trail and ride for about 2.5 miles to the Connecticut border. Otherwise, turn left on the rail-trail and ride for 2.5 miles back to the parking area.

RIDE 57 *GEORGE WASHINGTON MANAGEMENT AREA*

Take a day trip to the northwestern tip of Rhode Island to explore the single-track trails and narrow, rugged dirt roads in this large state park. You can warm up with a fun, scenic 1.5-mile loop on a single-track trail along the shore of a lake (with a beach). Afterward, head out on a moderately challenging ride using sections of the eight-mile Walkabout Trail and ten miles or so of interconnecting dirt roads. Less-experienced riders might stay on the roads.

Walkabout Trail sounds Australian because it is. The trail was built in 1965 by 300 Australian navy men waiting for their ship to be finished in a Rhode Island shipyard. Evidently someone in charge felt that several hundred sailors needed hard work. Their Lieutenant Unwin wrote of the undertaking: "Saturday night is barbeque night. Many of the local people and foresters come to sample our steaks. Residents of the area have been most hospitable and there will be many a lad who will be sorry to leave."

The trail was named after the well-known habit of Australian tribespeople, who simply get the urge to "go walkabout," which means roaming the land for days. It's a sentiment that should be familiar to many mountain bikers who get the urge to "go rideabout."

General location: The management area is located just off US 44 at the Connecticut border.

Elevation change: The terrain is rolling, with moderate climbs and descents on dirt roads, and some shorter, steeper climbs on the trails.

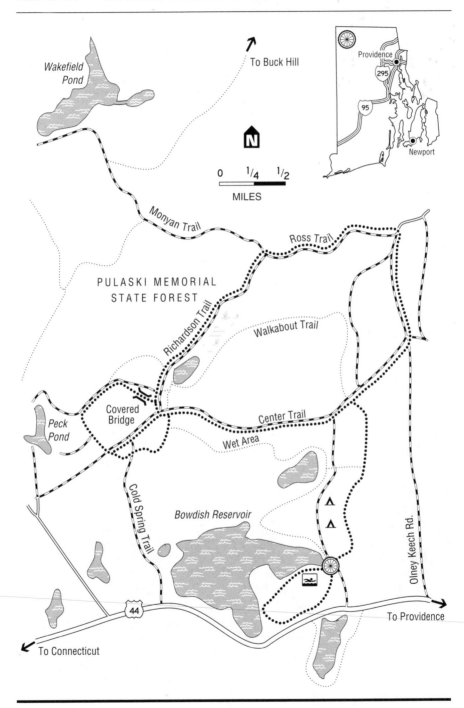

Wakefield
Pond

To Buck Hill

N

0   1/4   1/2
MILES

Providence
295
95
Newport

Monyan Trail

Ross Trail

PULASKI MEMORIAL
STATE FOREST

Richardson Trail

Walkabout Trail

Covered
Bridge

Peck
Pond

Center Trail

Wet Area

Cold Spring Trail

Bowdish Reservoir

Olney Keech Rd.

44

To Connecticut

To Providence

Season: This is a 4-season ride, if there is little snow. As always, for the trails' sake, avoid riding in wet or muddy conditions.

Services: All services are available along US 44. There are restrooms and a water fountain at the trailhead, and the park offers campsites from April through October 31 ($12 for non-residents).

Hazards: Watch for obstructions (such as small tree stumps) on the single-track trails, and an occasional vehicle or horseback rider on the dirt roads. Always yield to horseback riders.

Rescue index: At most you will be about 2 miles from help.

Land status: Trails and roads on public land.

Maps: A map is available at the headquarters, which is located on US 44 just past the access road to the trailhead.

Finding the trail: Take Exit 7 off Interstate 295 and go west on US 44. After about 12.5 miles you will pass a brown sign on the right: "George Washington Camping Area." Turn right at this sign and ride up the dirt road for about three-tenths of a mile. You will reach a gravel parking area on the left when you've made it to the beach at Bowdish Reservoir.

Sources of additional information:

Department of Environmental Management
Planning and Development
91 Hayes Street
Providence, RI 02908
(401) 277-2776

Treadheads, a local mountain biking club
(401) 232-5476

Notes on the trail: To take the 1.5-mile single-track loop near Bowdish Reservoir, ride down to the beach at the trailhead, veer left, and pick up the purple-blazed Angell Loop Trail running clockwise around the shore of the reservoir. After a half-mile or so, the trail will become smoother and will veer to the left, away from the reservoir. Follow it until it comes back out at the beach.

Now you can do a large loop, using both the 8-mile Walkabout Trail and dirt roads. Begin by picking up the Walkabout Trail just across the access road from the parking lot at the orange blazes. This trail is well marked by orange blazes. It also has 2-mile and 6-mile cutoff loops marked by blue and red blazes. You pass the blue-blazed cutoff trail on the left after about a half mile.

Next you come out on a wide dirt road (Center Trail). The Walkabout Trail becomes much more difficult on the other side of the road, so turn right on the road. (For a short loop, turn left on the road, then left again onto the access road.) At a 3-way intersection, turn left onto another dirt road. Then fork left onto the Ross Trail (another dirt road), and left again onto the Richardson Trail, a dirt road. (At this fork you can turn right for a longer ride into the Buck Hill Management Area.)

Negotiating a narrow trail. George Washington Management Area, West Gloucester, Rhode Island.

After about a mile on the Richardson Trail, you will pass a semi-hidden pond on the left, and just after it on the right a gated dirt road (Inner Border Trail) that takes you to a small covered bridge.

For a shorter ride, head straight on the Richardson Trail and soon turn left onto the Center Trail (another dirt road). For a longer ride, turn right onto the gated dirt road and ride through the covered bridge. Continue westward on the road, reaching Peck Pond in Pulaski Memorial State Park (which abuts this area), and then head east on either dirt roads or the orange-blazed Walkabout Trail once more (it intersects the road).

Before the last section of the Walkabout Trail (at the sign, "Cold Springs

Trail"), turn left on a cutoff road and pick up the Center Trail (dirt road) to avoid several wet areas on the single-track trail. The Center Trail forks right and at a 3-way intersection intersects the access road. Turn right and head south to the beach at Bowdish Reservoir.

RIDE 58 *LINCOLN WOODS STATE PARK*

This handsome park just outside Providence has 15 miles or so of single- and double-track trails winding through woods, past recreational fields, and around a large lake. Instead of extended ascents and descents, the area offers a fun network of shorter trails. There are flatter, smoother ones around the lake, and steep, rugged trails deeper in the woods.

One out-and-back trail leads to an overlook on a cliff above the lake. The park is also a popular swimming spot (at a designated beach), has several large playing fields (good for an impromptu game of bike frisbee), and a 2.5-mile paved loop road through the park that's popular among road riders.

A plaque at a site along the paved loop road informs visitors that this park was one of the nation's first managed forests. In 1895 its creator, W. W. Baily, waxed poetic about it: "In all seasons the landscape is ravishing, but never more so than when autumn has tinted the leaves with crimson gold or claret . . . It is not difficult to fancy oneself transferred to a locality remote from settlements, yet by climbing the hills to the north, one can see smiling villages and the evidence of thrift and civilization." Climb those hills.

General location: The park is in Lincoln, just north of Providence, and just off RI 146.

Elevation change: Although the area is relatively flat, trails climb and descend, and the riding is sometimes made more challenging by loose terrain.

Season: Good drainage makes this a 4-season ride. As always, though, avoid riding on trails in wet conditions.

Services: In summer, water, restrooms, and a concession stand are available on the beach at the lake. All other services are available in Lincoln and Providence.

Hazards: Watch for motorists and road cyclists on the paved loop road through the park. Also, because the park is close to several cities, it attracts many visitors; slow down on downhills and yield to horseback riders.

Rescue index: Well-traveled roads and homes surround the park.

Land status: State park trails.

Maps: There is a large, detailed map on a board on the paved road in the park. From the entrance, turn left to reach it. Otherwise, the map in this book is the best published map.

Finding the trail: From Interstate 295, take Exit 9A onto RI 146, heading south

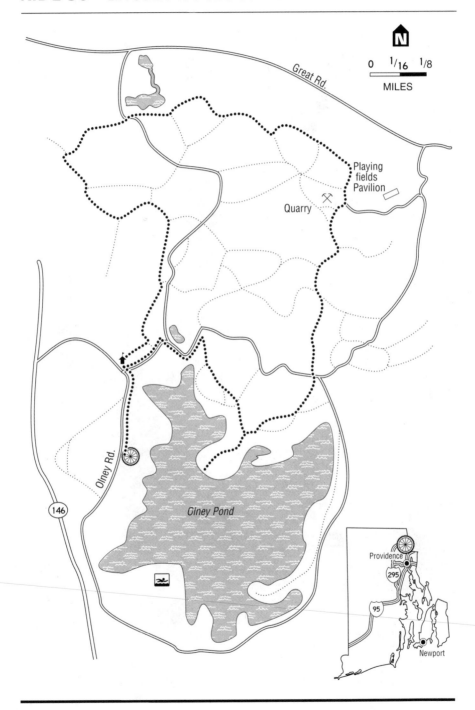

Great Rd.

N

0   1/16   1/8
MILES

Playing
fields
Pavilion

Quarry

Olney Rd.

146

Olney Pond

Providence

295

95

Newport

Finding a line. Lincoln Woods, Lincoln, Rhode Island.

toward Providence. After 4 miles, watch for exit signs for the park. Follow these green signs and then fork right at the park entrance and you will reach a large paved parking lot on the left. *Note:* The park has begun charging a small fee for vehicle parking. If you want to avoid the fee, just park outside the area and ride in.

Sources of additional information: Treadheads, a mountain biking club, sponsors rides that meet in the parking lot, even in winter. Phone: (401) 232-5476. Also try the following:

B&B Cycle & Sport
541 Power Road
Pawtucket, RI 02860
(401) 725-2830

Department of Environmental Management
Planning and Development
91 Hayes Street
Providence, RI 02908
(401) 277-2776

Notes on the trail: The paved road that loops through the middle of the park divides the trails into an "inner" loop and an "outer" loop. Both areas are actually networks of trails that hook up across the paved road. The inner loop is easier riding.

To begin a counterclockwise ride on the outer loop, fork off the paved park road just left of the park's entrance, onto a single-track trail. Follow this trail as it rolls through the woods, circumventing the park. You will cross a dead-end paved access road, pass an old stone house foundation, arrive at a playing field and pavilion on the other side of the park, and approach the lake. Be sure to take the side trail that crosses a peninsula to reach an overlook above the lake.

Glossary

This short list of terms does not contain all the words used by mountain bike enthusiasts when discussing their sport. But it should serve as an introduction to the lingo you'll hear on the trails.

ATB all-terrain bike; this, like "fat-tire bike," is another name for a mountain bike

ATV all-terrain vehicle; this usually refers to the loud, fume-spewing three- or four-wheeled motorized vehicles you will not enjoy meeting on the trail—except of course if you crash and have to hitch a ride out on one

bladed refers to a dirt road that has been smoothed out by the use of a wide blade on earth-moving equipment; "blading" gets rid of the teeth-chattering, much-cursed washboards found on so many dirt roads after heavy vehicle use

blaze a mark on a tree made by chipping away a piece of the bark, usually done to designate a trail; such trails are sometimes described as "blazed"

BLM Bureau of Land Management, an agency of the federal government

buffed used to describe a very smooth trail

catching air taking a jump in such a way that both wheels of the bike are off the ground at the same time

clean while this can be used to describe what you and your bike *won't* be after following many trails, the term is most often used as a verb to denote the action of pedaling a tough section of trail successfully

deadfall a tangled mass of fallen trees or branches

diversion ditch a usually narrow, shallow ditch dug across or around a trail; funneling the water in this manner keeps it from destroying the trail

double-track the dual tracks made by a jeep or other vehicle, with grass or weeds or rocks between; the mountain biker can therefore ride in either of the tracks, but will of course find that whichever is chosen, and no matter how many times one

	changes back and forth, the other track will appear to offer smoother travel
dugway	a steep, unpaved, switchbacked descent
feathering	using a light touch on the brake lever, hitting it lightly many times rather than very hard or locking the brake
four-wheel-drive	this refers to any vehicle with drive-wheel capability on all four wheels (a jeep, for instance, as compared to a two-wheel-drive passenger car), or to a rough road or trail that requires four-wheel-drive capability (or a *one*-wheel drive mountain bike!) to traverse it
game trail	the usually narrow trail made by deer, elk, or other game
gated	everyone knows what a gate is, and how many variations exist upon this theme; well, if a trail is described as "gated" it simply has a gate across it; don't forget that the rule is if you find a gate closed, close it behind you; if you find one open, leave it that way
Giardia	shorthand for *Giardia lamblia,* known as the "backpacker's bane" until we mountain bikers appropriated it; this is a waterborne parasite that begins its life cycle when swallowed, and one to four weeks later has its host (you) bloated, vomiting, shivering with chills, and living in the bathroom; the disease can be avoided by "treating" (purifying) the water you acquire along the trail (see "Hitting the Trail")
gnarly	thankfully a term used less and less these days, it refers to tough trails
hammer	to ride very hard
hardpack	used to describe a trail in which the dirt surface is packed down hard; such trails make for good and fast riding, and very painful landings; bikers most often use "hardpack" as both a noun and adjective, and "hardpacked" as an adjective only (the grammar lesson will help you when diagramming sentences in camp)
jeep road, jeep trail	a rough road or trail which requires four-wheel-drive capability (or a horse or mountain bike) to traverse it
kamikaze	while this once referred primarily to those Japanese fliers who quaffed a glass of saki, then flew off as human bombs in suicide missions against U.S. naval vessels, it has more

recently been applied to the idiot mountain bikers who, far less honorably, scream down hiking trails, endangering the physical and mental safety of the walking, biking, and equestrian traffic they meet; deck guns were necessary to stop the Japanese kamikaze pilots, but a bike pump or walking staff in the spokes is sufficient for the current-day kamikazes who threaten to get us all kicked off the trails

multi-purpose	a BLM designation of land that is open to multi-purpose use; mountain biking is allowed
out-and-back	a ride in which you will return on the same trail you pedaled out; while this might sound far more boring than a loop route, many trails look very different when pedaled in the opposite direction
portage	to carry your bike on your person
quads	bikers use this term to refer both to the extensor muscle in the front of the thigh (which is separated into four parts), and to USGS maps; the expression "Nice quads!" refers always to the former, however, except in those instances when the speaker is an engineer
runoff	rainwater or snowmelt
signed	a signed trail is denoted by signs in place of blazes
single-track	a single track through grass or brush or over rocky terrain, often created by deer, elk, or backpackers; single-track riding is some of the best fun around
slickrock	the rock-hard, compacted sandstone that is *great* to ride and even prettier to look at; you'll appreciate it more if you think of it as a petrified sand dune or seabed, and if the rider before you hasn't left tire marks (from unnecessary skidding) or granola bar wrappers behind
snowmelt	runoff produced by the melting of snow
snowpack	unmelted snow accumulated over weeks or months of winter, or over years in high-mountain terrain
spur	a road or trail that intersects the main trail you're following
technical	terrain that is difficult to ride due not to its grade (steepness) but because of obstacles—rocks, logs, ledges, loose soil . . .
topo	short for topographical map, the kind that shows both

linear distance *and* elevation gain and loss; "topo" is pronounced with both vowels long

trashed a trail that has been destroyed (same term used no matter what has destroyed it . . . cattle, horses, or even mountain bikers riding when the ground was too wet)

two-wheel-drive this refers to any vehicle with drive-wheel capability on only two wheels (a passenger car, for instance, compared to a jeep), or to an easy road or trail that a two-wheel-drive vehicle could traverse

water bar an earth, rock, or wooden structure that funnels water off trails

washboarded a road with many ridges spaced closely together, like the ripples on a washboard; these make for very rough riding, and even worse driving in a car or jeep

wilderness area land that is officially set aside by the Federal Government to remain *natural*—pure, pristine, and untrammeled by any vehicle, including mountain bikes; though mountain bikes had not been born in 1964 (when the United States Congress passed the Wilderness Act, establishing the National Wilderness Preservation system) they are considered a "form of mechanical transport" and are thereby excluded; in short, stay out

wind chill a reference to the wind's cooling effect upon exposed flesh; for example, if the temperature is 10 degrees Fahrenheit and the wind is blowing at 20 miles per hour, the wind-chill effect (that is, the actual temperature to which your skin reacts) is *minus* 32 degrees; if you are riding in wet conditions things are even worse, for the wind-chill effect would then be *minus 74 degrees!*

windfall anything (trees, limbs, brush, fellow bikers) blown down by the wind

PAUL ANGIOLILLO is a much-published freelance writer and editor. His articles have appeared in the *Boston Globe, Bicycling, Business Week, Omni, Metrosports, Dirt Rag,* and many other newspapers and magazines. He is also the author of another book in the America by Mountain Bike series, *The Mountain Biker's Guide to Northern New England.* Paul began mountain biking at the age of eight, when he rode his first bicycle into a large ditch in the woods behind his home. Later, he dodged potholes in Boston, where he served as president of the Boston Area Bicycle Coalition. Now he gets his thrills exploring old fire roads and trails throughout New England.

Dennis Coello's America By Mountain Bike Series

Happy Trails

Hop on your mountain bike and let our guidebooks take you on America's classic trails and rides. These "where-to" books are published jointly by Falcon Press and Menasha Ridge Press and written by local biking experts. Twenty regional books will blanket the country when the series is complete.

Choose from an assortment of rides—easy rambles to all-day treks. Guides contain helpful trail and route descriptions, mountain bike shop listings; and interesting facts on area history. Each trail is described in terms of difficulty, scenery, condition, length, and elevation change. The guides also explain trail hazards, nearby services and ranger stations, how much water to bring, and what kind of gear to pack.

So before you hit the trail, grab one of our guidebooks to help make your outdoor adventures safe and memorable.

Call or write
Falcon Press or Menasha Ridge Press
Falcon Press
P.O. Box 1718, Helena, MT 59624
1-800-582-2665
Menasha Ridge Press
3169 Cahaba Heights Road, Birmingham, AL 35243
1-800-247-9437

FALCONGUIDES   *Perfect for every outdoor adventure!*

FISHING

Angler's Guide to Alaska
Angler's Guide to Minnesota
Angler's Guide to Montana
Beartooth Fishing Guide

FLOATING

Floater's Guide to Colorado
Floater's Guide to Missouri
Floater's Guide to Montana

HIKING

Hiker's Guide to Alaska
Hiker's Guide to Alberta
Hiker's Guide to Arizona
Hiker's Guide to California
Hiker's Guide to Colorado
Hiker's Guide to Hot Springs
    in the Pacific Northwest
Hiker's Guide to Idaho
Hiker's Guide to Missouri
Hiker's Guide to Montana
Hiker's Guide to Montana's
    Continental Divide Trail
Hiker's Guide to Nevada
Hiker's Guide to New Mexico
Hiker's Guide to Oregon
Hiker's Guide to Texas
Hiker's Guide to Utah
Hiker's Guide to Virginia
Hiker's Guide to Washington
Hiker's Guide to Wyoming
Hiking Softly, Hiking Safely
Trail Guide to Glacier National Park

MOUNTAIN BIKING

Mountain Biker's Guide to Arizona
Mountain Biker's Guide to
    Central Appalachia

Mountain Biker's Guide to
    Northern New England
Mountain Biker's Guide to
    Southern California

ROCKHOUNDING

Rockhound's Guide to Arizona
Rockhound's Guide to Montana

SCENIC DRIVING

Arizona Scenic Drives
Back Country Byways
California Scenic Drives
Oregon Scenic Drives
Scenic Byways
Scenic Byways II
Trail of the Great Bear
Traveler's Guide to the Oregon Trail

WILDLIFE VIEWING GUIDES

Arizona Wildlife Viewing Guide
California Wildlife Viewing Guide
Colorado Wildlife Viewing Guide
Idaho Wildlife Viewing Guide
Indiana Wildlife Viewing Guide
Montana Wildlife Viewing Guide
North Carolina Wildlife Viewing Guide
North Dakota Wildlife Viewing Guide
Oregon Wildlife Viewing Guide
Texas Wildlife Viewing Guide
Utah Wildlife Viewing Guide
Washington Wildlife Viewing Guide

PLUS—

Birder's Guide to Montana
Hunter's Guide to Montana
Recreation Guide to
    California National Forests
Recreation Guide to
    Washington National Forests

Falcon Press Publishing Co.   •   Call toll-free 1-800-582-2665

The Mountain Bike Way to Knowledge is through William Nealy

No other great Zen master approaches William Nealy in style or originality. His handwritten text, signature cartoons, and off-beat sense of humor have made him a household name among bikers. His expertise, acquired through years of meditation (and some crash and burn), enables him to translate hard-learned reflexes and instinctive responses into his unique, easy-to-understand drawings. Anyone who wants to learn from the master (and even those who don't) will get a good laugh.

Mountain Bike!
A Manual of Beginning to Advanced Technique

The ultimate mountain bike book for the totally honed! Master the techniques of mountain biking and have a good laugh while logging miles with Nealy.

Soft cover, 172 pages, 7" by 10"
Cartoon illustrations
$12.95

The Mountain Bike Way of Knowledge

This is the first compendium of mountain bike "insider" knowledge ever published. Between the covers of this book are the secrets of wheelie turns, log jumps, bar hops, dog evasion techniques, and much more! Nealy shares his wisdom with beginner and expert alike in this self-help manual.

Soft cover, 128 pages, 8" by 5 1/2"
Cartoon illustrations
$6.95

From Menasha Ridge Press
1-800-247-9437